Your Personal Mega Power For Love, Luck, Prosperity

By

Maria D'Andrea MsD, D.D., DRH

Your Personal Mega Power Spells

© 2005 Rev. Mária Solomon

Your Personal Mega Power Spells

© Copyright 2000 and 2011 by Maria D'Andrea

ISBN-10: 1606111051
ISBN-13: 978-1606111055

Drawings and illustrations are by Brother Francis Revels-Bey, Howard Solomon and the author. Covers by Tim Swartz.

Layout and editorial of original edition by Howard Solomon.

All Rights Reserved. No part of this book may be reproduced, stored in a retrieval system, or transmitted, in any form or by any means, electronic, mechanical, photocopying, recording, or otherwise, without prior permission of the author and publisher. Manufactured in the United States.

Timothy Green Beckley, Publisher

dba Inner Light Publications

Free Subscription To Weekly Online Newsletter –

www.ConspiracyJournal.Com

Your Personal Mega Power Spells

Other Books By The Author:

- Psychic Vibrations of Crystals, Gems and Stones
- New Age Formulary
- Helping Yourself With Magickal Oils A-Z
- Heaven Sent Money Spells
- How To Terminate Stress With Meditation Strategies
- Love And Light In The Garden Of God – Collective Writings

PLUS NUMEROUS DVD SETS – SEE BACK OF THIS BOOK

For Services and Products Contact:

Rev. Maria D'Andrea
www.mariadandrea.com

DEDICATION

To Howard and my family,

For all their love, support and enthusiasm for this book.

May they continue to receive their Blessings with love.

FOREWORD

By Rick Holecek

Wicca and witchcraft have been portrayed as very scary or completely unbelievable in many of the Hollywood movies. You may be surprised to learn that Wicca is very "people-friendly" and often results in positive, tangible outcomes.

Reverend Maria D'Andrea has been studying various religions, mysticism and the occult for over 40 years. By using her gifts and knowledge to aid others, Reverend Maria has earned the respect of many witches, ministers, shaman, and business professionals. I have personally witnessed her use of Wiccan rituals to achieve numerous goals including attracting money and increasing business opportunities. The results have been amazing.

In her book, "Do It Yourself Wicca", Reverend Maria will teach you how to help yourself, your friends, and your family by uncovering the most effective Wiccan methods. Her book explains the basic principles of Wicca and dives right in to how to get positive results. Reverend Maria's books are known to be direct and to the point. The quick results you will achieve from using this book will increase your faith in yourself and in the spiritual realm.

Enjoy your spiritual journey.

ACKNOWLEDGEMENTS

I would like to thank the following contributors to this book:

<u>My friend Howard</u> - who balances my spiritual and physical realities with **love**, compassion, kindness and understanding. Howard is a very dynamic motivator in his profession and with me, as a life partner.

<u>My two sons</u> - who truly connect with nature:

<u>Rob D'Andrea</u> - for his creative approach to life and his expertise in manifesting his heart's desires. He is an inspiring **S**age.

<u>Rick Holecek</u> - who playfully balances both realities with humor and astute wisdom in a forever-changing world. a true **W**izard..

<u>Gina Holecek</u> – Rick's other half and a spiritually expanding being, dancing in the energy fields.

<u>My mother, Maria Berde</u> - an angel when it came to helping to get things back in motion, also a gifted writer among her many professions.

<u>My father, Lichtig László</u> - for his loving advice, information and never ending enthusiasm (Márta's brother).

<u>My friend, Robert Krachenfels</u> - an extremely positive person. An original creative thinker, who lives his life to the fullest from his heart.

<u>My Spiritual Brother, Francis Revels-Bey</u> - also my colleague. We have been on numerous Spiritual adventures together. As a long term Principle Teacher of Tai Chi and a well-known spiritualist, he has contributed to this book from multi levels of existence.

Your Personal Mega Power Spells

Introduction

Witchcraft is an active religion, practiced by countless people. Just as any other religion, there are positive and negative individuals. The religion itself is a practical, nature based, positive belief system, combining religion and magick.

No longer underground, the occult/mystery secrets are more out in the open for all to utilize. God gave everyone the ability and the choice to incorporate it into everyday life.

The religion of Witchcraft is also known as the Craft. It is a combination of science and magick. Witches through psychic and magick practices gain positive, practical ends. The religion varies from coven to coven It is a creative and diverse belief system. Witch is based on varied schools of thought such as: Traditional; Celtic; Dianic; Saxon; Alexandrian; Solitary and Gardenerian.

You do not need to be a witch to be able to utilize the ancient methods of magick. They have worked for centuries and will continue to do so for many more.

Some formulae or spells in this book are ancient, some modern, and many are mine. The key to magick is to understand how the Universal Laws work. Then work with them to cause specific changes and influences in your life.

These methods work in the same manner as science: Cause and Effect. If you do something and it consistently works, you will repeat it. If it does not, you do not use it again. Since these methods are still around since ancient times, it assures you of a positive outcome. You need only to add your will power and belief or knowing. Your emotions and attitude, what you want or need are all important. Work with realities, the physical and non-physical. It is essential. You are not just doing magick, you are part of the magick itself as a practitioner.

As neophytes and adepts all know, there is Power in Positive Focus.

You will work with spell crafting, divination, nature and rituals, among other magickal forms.

Through years of experience with the psychic and magickal fields, I have put together powerful, yet easily workable formulae. Practitioners of all levels can utilize them. This book is geared for solitary work, but can be adapted to group practice.

I suggest you keep a Book of Shadows, also know as a "Grimoire". This is a magician's personal record of information. What spells worked, folklore, divination methods, symbols, alchemy, elemental magick, dreams and talisman. Any information relevant to you for psychic/magick work. It is very personal and private. Some pass their book down from generation to generation only. It can be invaluable through years of work. As an example: To give insight; spells you created; short cuts you have found that work; and what to avoid the next time.

When working any spell, first write down what you want or desire. <u>Then</u>, realize that you will not have to "want" anymore. As you ask, the Universe supplies. Next, thank the Universe (God/Goddess or whatever term you use). Giving thanks is very important. It also tells the Universe that you trust it and know it works. Always phrase everything in the present tense.

Once you start to manifest, remember that your belief is very important. The more you manifest your goals, the easier it becomes. It really seems to go in steps when you get your goal.

First time you achieve our goal - There is some doubt, you say to yourself - did <u>I</u> do that? - and you will justify it from a logical point of view.

Second time it happens - You start to believe.

Third time - Now you believe.

Fourth time - It starts to manifest - to bring your goal to you faster and faster.

Fifth time - As you focus on your goal, it is already manifesting.

This book was written more to give you an ability to manifest immediately, than to focus

on the history of Wicca.

Begin to relax, have fun and take action!

Live the life of magick and your life will become magickally successful!

Love & Light

Maria D'Andrea

Your Personal Mega Power Spells

INVOCATION

FOR

PROTECTION

by

Maria D'Andrea

I now invoke the Triple Goddess,

Deity of ancient times,

I now invoke the God of Hunting,

For the power of his might.

Protect me while I weave my spells,

Make sacred the space I walk on,

Be with me as I go in Light,

Blessed Be the God and Goddess.

So Mote It Be.

Suggested Protection prior to **any** work

Your Personal Mega Power Spells

Table of Contents

OTHER BOOKS BY THE AUTHOR: IV
FOR SERVICES AND PRODUCTS CONTACT: IV
DEDICATION V
FOREWORD VI
ACKNOWLEDGEMENTS VII
INTRODUCTION VIII
INVOCATION FOR PROTECTION X
TABLE OF CONTENTS XI

CHAPTER ONE 1
   WITCHCRAFT -BELIEF, MAGICK AND SCIENCE 1
      WITCHCRAFT - Belief, Magick and Science 2

CHAPTER TWO 3
   YOUR TOOLS OF POWER 3
      YOU ARE THE TOOL!!! 4

CHAPTER THREE 7
   SYMBOLISM AND CHARTS OF THE MAGICKAL WORLD 7
      CHARTS AND SYMBOLS 10
      SYMBOLS FOR THE FIVE ELEMENTS 10
      ELEMENT CORRESPONDENCES 11
      CONTINUED-CORRESPONDENCES 11
      VARIOUS TOOLS 12
      PURPOSE 12
      CORRESPONDENCE of MAGICK and ASTROLOGY 13
      PLANETARY ACTIVITIES 13
      ASTROLOGY and ALCHEMY 14
      CHAKRAS AND COLORS 15
      COLORS 15
      ELEMENT-BODY- COLOR CORRESPONDENCES 16
      COLORS AND MUSIC 17
      THE WITCHES' SABBATS 18
      WHEEL OF THE YEAR 19
      SOME BASIC HOLIDAY MEANINGS 19
      ESBATS 20
      GODDESS CORRESPONDENCES 20
      HORNED GOD-CORRESPONDENCES 21
      THE SEVEN DIRECIONS 21
      SYMBOLS AND USES 26
      ALCHEMY 27
      CORRESPONDENCE CHART 28
      SEAL OF THE SUN 29

CHAPTER FOUR 30
   PROTECTION AND BLESSINGS - YOUR UNSEEN FORCES 30
      A CHILDS' PROTECTION PRAYER/SPELL 31

Your Personal Mega Power Spells

BLESSING FOR A CHILD	*32*
CIRCLE OF SELF-PROTECTION	*32*
HOME PROTECTION AND BLESSING	*33*
BLESSING UPON A JOB	*34*
DOLL OF PROTECTION - For House	*35*
THE ALTAR OF PROTECTION RITUAL	*37*
PROTECTION BATH	*38*
SWORD OF PROTECTION	*38*
A BLESSING CIRCLE RITUAL	*40*
ELIXIR OF THE EARTHLY FORCE	*41*
INVOCATION TO THE GODDESS	*41*
TO HAVE COMPUTERS BREAK DOWN LESS FREQUENTLY- A Protection Spell	*42*
PROTECT YOURSELF FROM NEGATIVE COWORKERS	*42*
BLESSING TREE SPELL	*42*
PROTECTION CORD	*43*
CAR SECURITY	*43*
HOUSE BLESSING RITUAL	*44*
ELEMENTAL WATER SPELL	*45*
BLESSING THE PLANTS, FIELDS, CROPS	*45*
PROTECTION RITUAL	*46*
BLESSING PETS-ANIMALS	*47*
PINE-WIND DANCE-Protection	*48*
PROTECTIVE AMULET	*48*
RUNE BINDING FOR PROTECTION	*51*
INCANTATION FOR A WATER PROTECTION SPELL	*51*
GENERAL BLESSING	*52*
PROTECTIVE CHARM	*53*
ANCIENT ELVES WOOD PROTECTION SPELL	*54*
STONE OF SAFETY DURING TRAVEL	*55*
TO WARD OFF NEGATIVE INFLUENCES IN YOUR HOME	*56*
HEX BREAKING	*56*
PROTECTION FROM ILLNESS	*56*
SHIELDING	*57*
AVOID DANGER	*58*
PEACEFUL HOME	*58*
BRINGS PROTECTION AND BLESSING	*58*
TO STOP T.V. INTERFERENCE	*59*
TO CANCEL DEPRESSION	*59*
PROTECTION AND HEX BREAKING	*59*
EXORCISM	*59*
SEND AWAY EVIL	*60*
HOUSE PROTECTION	*60*
GOURDS FOR PROTECTION	*60*
HOUSE BLESSING KIT	*60*
BLACK DOLL OF PROTECTION	*61*
BELL AND CANDLE	*62*
HEX-BREAKING TOAD	*62*
UNCROSSING RITUAL	*63*
PROTECTION AT WORK	*64*
BANISH NEGATIVE PHONE CALLS	*64*
UNHEXING	*65*
UNHEXING BAG	*65*
SAFETY	*65*
THE GUARDIAN	*66*
TOBACCO MAGICK	*66*
PROTECT YOUR LUGGAGE	*66*
KEEPS NEGATIVITY OUT AND WEAKENS NEGATIVE PEOPLE	*67*
ANCIENT PROTECTION RITUAL	*67*
PROTECTION OF MARS	*67*
PROTECTION OF WATER CRAFT- BOATS-SURF BOARDS, ETC.	*67*

Your Personal Mega Power Spells

- SHIELDING 68
- TO SPOT AN ENEMY 69
- HEIGHTEN ABILITY OF PSYCHIC LEVELS 69

CHAPTER FIVE 70
- FORMULAE FOR ATTRACTING LOVE AND ROMANCE 70
  - RITUAL TO BRING LOVE IN 71
  - TIGER LUST 72
  - LOVE MAGNET 73
  - SENSUAL VIBRATIONS 73
  - LUST OF THE GODS 73
  - MAGNETIC POWER-TO ATTRACT MEN 73
  - MAGNETIC POWER-TO ATTRACT WOMEN 74
  - FIDELITY IN LOVE 74
  - ELIXIR OF LOVE 74
  - COLOR OF LOVE 74
  - FRIENDSHIP 74
  - COMMERCIAL LOVE POTIONS 75
  - EXCITEMENT OF LOVE 75
  - EROTIC ATTRACTION SPELL 76
  - RUNIC SIGIL FOR FIDELITY 77
  - COME TO ME 78
  - POPPET OF LOVE-NEW 78
  - ORRIS ROOT RITUAL 79
  - INCREASE LOVE 80
  - PASSION 80
  - EGYPTIAN LOVE TALISMAN 81
  - WOMEN ONLY-LOVE/LUST SPELL 82
  - TREE OF FERTILITY 82
  - FAIRIES-BRING REALMS OF LOVE 83
  - BUTTERFLY SPELL-TO CHANGE A SITUATION 83
  - HUNGARIAN LOVE MAGICK 84
  - PEACH SPELL FOR LOVE 84
  - SALAMANDER POWER 85
  - LOVE SPELL 85
  - ATTRECT NEW FRIENDS 86
  - LUSTFUL LOVE OF THE AGES 86
  - LUSTY MARS 86
  - THE ORCHID SPELL 87
  - THE GENIE SPELL 87
  - AIR AND EARTH MAGICK 88
  - FLOWER OF LOVE - To Make Love Grow 89
  - EROTIC LOVE TALISMAN 89
  - POWER OF DRACOS 90
  - IMAGE MAGICK 90
  - SPELLS OF LOVE 91
  - FAIRY FIRE SPELL 91
  - HAPPINESS IN LOVE 92
  - CIRCLE OF LOVE 92
  - GINGER OF POWER 93
  - DRAGON SPELL OF LOVE 93
  - ALTAR OF ROSES 94
  - SPELLCRAFT OF THE MAGI 95
  - TREE SPIRITS - ATTRACTING YOUR MATE 95
  - LEMON WISH FOR FRIENDSHIP 96
  - STOP INFIDELITY 97
  - CANDLE OF DESIRE 97
  - LOVE AND HARMONY 98
  - INSPIRE LOVE 98
  - BRING NEW LOVERS 98

Your Personal Mega Power Spells

- *SPIRIT OF LUSTFULL PASSION* 99
- *MANDRAKE-YOUR HEART'S DESIRE TO COME BACK* 99
- *MOUNTAIN MAGICK* 100
- *PAN-EARTHLY LOVE* 100
- *LANTERN OF LOVE* 101
- *LOVE ATTRACTION TALISMAN* 102
- *WHEN LOVE MUST COME TO YOU* 102
- *TO GET SOMEONE TO SHOW LOVE* 103
- *TO COOL OFF TEMPERS* 103
- *MAGICK MIRROR* 103
- *FOR SOMEONE TO COME TO YOU IN A POSOTIVE WAY* 104
- *RABBITS' FOOT FOR LOVE* 104
- *EYE CONTACT SPELL- TO BRING SOMEONE IN* 104

CHAPTER SIX 105
- DRAWING THE CORNUCOPIA OF LUCK INTO YOUR LIFE 105
  - *LUCKY RABBITS' FOOT KIT* 107
  - *LUCKY MONEY MAGNET* 107
  - *SHOWERS OF GOLD* 108
  - *IRISH LUCK* 108
  - *WINNING HORSE RACES* 108
  - *GOOD FORTUNE* 109
  - *ORANGES OF LUCK* 109
  - *LUCKY LIFE* 109
  - *LUCKY PLANET* 110
  - *GEM OF POWER* 110
  - *ALL-PURPOSE LUCK* 110
  - *LUCKY BATH* 111
  - *LUCKY NUMBERS* 111
  - *LUCK AND GAMBLING* 111
  - *LUCKY STONE* 112
  - *ELEPHANT ENERGY* 112
  - *WORD OF POWER* 112
  - *LUCK ATTRACTION* 113
  - *BALL OF LUCK* 113
  - *LUCKY BOWL* 114
  - *HOLLY* 114
  - *FREYA-GODDESS OF LUCK* 114
  - *THE FAIRY WOODS* 115
  - *ALTAR OF LUCK* 116
  - *HELP OF THE GNOMES* 117
  - *LUCKY BATH* 117
  - *SPIRIT OF THE EARTH* 118
  - *THE POWER OF BLACK* 118
  - *LUCKY OILS* 120
  - *WISHING CANDLE* 120
  - *LUCKY TALISMAN* 120
  - *A CHARM TO DRAW LUCK IN GAMBLING* 121
  - *DOUBLE POWER* 122
  - *TALISMANIC ENERGY* 122
  - *YOUR OWN PERSONAL BAG* 123
  - *LUCKY NUMBER BAG – FOR GAMES OF CHANCE* 124
  - *GAMBLING HAND* 125
  - *BINGO BAG* 125
  - *STONE POWER* 126
  - *FOUR LEAF CLOVER AND EGYPTIAN SCARAB FOR LUCK* 126
  - *BRING LUCK* 127
  - *LUCKY NUMBER CANDLE* 127
  - *FAST LUCK* 127
  - *LUCKY GAMBLERS WASH* 128

Your Personal Mega Power Spells

GOOD LUCK IN ALL THINGS 128
HOME OF THE ELVES 128
FLOOR WASH 128
PHOENIX SPELL 129
BINGO 129
FAST LUCK DOLL 130
NECKLACE OF PAN 131
FAIRY STONE 131
GOOD LUCK CHARM 132
YOUR LUCKY SPELL 132
WALNUT SPIRITS 132
RITUAL FOR GAMBLING 133
FLOWER OF LUCK 133
MAGICK BEANS 133
LUCK IN BUSINESS 133
NEW JOB 133
ALL-PURPOSE LUCK 134
WINNING STREAK 134
BURNING BUSH 134
LUCK AT ANY RACE 134
INCREASE YOUR LUCK 136
CANDLE MAGIC-LUCK IN LOVE 137
LUCKY NUMBERS-WITH SPIRIT'S HELP 138
FAST LUCKY NUMBERS 139
BLACK CAT OF LUCK 139
LUCK IN A NEW VENTURE 139
LUCK IN TRAVEL 140
LUCK DRAWING 141
CHARM 142
BINGO BAG OF LUCK 142
DRAGON'S LUCK 143
ADDED POWER 144
PERSONAL LUCK 144
MAGNETIC LUCK WITH MONEY 145
INCREASE BUSINESS 146
CHARM FOR LUCK IN COURT 146
LUCKY CANDLE OF LOVE, SEX AND ROMANCE 147
LUCKY DUCK 148
STAR LUCK 148
ROOT TALISMAN 148
FAIRY DOLL LUCK 149

CHAPTER SEVEN **150**
CREATING POSITIVE CASH FLOW TO ENHANCE YOUR PROSPERITY 150
CAULDRON OF MONEY 151
AFFIRM 152
TALISMAN FOR BUSINESS AND SUCCESS 153
PROSPEROUS HOME 154
BRING MORE MONEY TO YOUR BUSINESS 154
MONEY GROWING RITUAL 154
TREASURE HUNTING 154
INCREASE BUSINESS, MONEY OR TO GET A RAISE 154
MONEY ATTRACTION 155
MONEY TREE SPELL 155
CANDLE OF DIANA 156
SEASHORE SPELL FOR PROSPERITY 157
PROSPERITY MAGNET 157
RABBIT'S FOOT FOR MONEY 157
PROSPERITY DOLL 158
MONEY NECKLACE 158

Your Personal Mega Power Spells

ALL PURPOSE PROSPERITY RITUAL *159*
TREASURE MAP FOR MONEY IN BUSINESS *159*
AFFIRMATION FOR MONEY *160*
MONEY TO COME TO YOU *160*
ALL PURPOSE CANDLE SPELL *161*
PROSPERITY POWER *162*
BLODENWEDD'S RITUAL *163*
RITUAL-MONEY TO COME IN *164*
AFFIRMATION *165*
TO SELL PROPERTY *165*
TO GET A JOB *165*
MONEY AND LUCK *165*
BUSINES/MONEY CIRCLE *166*
MONEY PATH FOR WEALTH *166*
MONEY DOLL RITUAL - FOR PLAYING NUMBERS *166*
MONEY AND PROSPERITY RITUAL *168*

CHAPTER EIGHT **170**

A HEALTHY LIFE EQUALS A BALANCED LIFE 170
EXCESS WATER *171*
CUTS AND BRUISES *171*
HEIGHTEN ABILITY TO HEAL *172*
GOLD POWER TO HEAL *172*
THE VISION OF GNOMES *173*
BACKACHE PREVENTION *174*
BENEFICIA L NUTRIENTS *174*
TO BANISH PAIN *175*
HEALING SEA SPELL *176*
THROAT PROBLEMS-OR PAINFUL AREAS *176*
CURE DEPRESSION-AVOID FEVER *177*
ILLNESS PREVENTION *177*
TOBACCO-DIGESTION AID *178*
METABOLISM *178*
RED STRENGTH *178*
IMMUNE SYSTEM *179*
ELFIN NECKLACE *179*
MOON HEALING *179*
HOUSE OF HEALING *180*
THE SPELL OF IVY *180*
MEDICINE BAG-HEALING *180*
MERCURY'S TREE *180*
STONE OF HEALING *181*
ALTAR WORK *181*
ONION SPELLS *182*
PEPPER SPELL *183*
HEALTH TALISMAN *183*
SLEEP AID *184*
PEACEFUL SLEEP *184*
HEALING CANDLE *184*
HEALING ELIXIR *185*
ACORN SPELL *185*
DISTANT HEALING *186*
SEA MAGIC FOR HEALTH *186*

CHAPTER NINE **187**

DIVINING LIFE'S PURPOSES WITH POSITIVE MAGICK 187
YES/NO CARD SPREAD *188*
WATER DIVINATION *189*
DIVINATION FOR LUCKY NUMBERS *189*
PSYCHOMETRY *191*

Your Personal Mega Power Spells

    ALWAYS WASH YOUR HANDS AFTER! 192
    EXERCISES FOR DEVELOPING SENSITIVITY FOR PSYCHOMETRY 193
    ESTABLISHING CONNECTIONS WITH THE GOD/GODDESS 193
    DREAM WORK 194
    FIRE SCRYING 194

CHAPTER TEN 195
  HOW TO FAX YOUR HEART'S DESIRES - THROUGH MEDITATION AND VISUALIZATION 195
    ALPHA REALITY 199
    VISUALIZATION FOR ANY DESIRE 200
    MEDITATION TO GAIN INFORMATION 201
    MAGICKAL MEDITATION 201
    VISUALIZATION TO RECHARGE 202
    TO IMPROVE A SITUATION 203
    VISUALIZATION FOR A MAGICKAL WORK SPACE 204
    GOAL VISUALIZATION 204
    FINDING YOUR DIRECTION 205
    CANDLE RITUAL FOR VISUALIZATION 206
    TO CHANGE YOURSELF 207
    OAK TREE MEDITATION 208
    HOW TO RELATE TO TREES 208
    MEDITATION ROOM 209
    DRAGON MEDITATION 210
    TREASURE CHEST MEDITATION 211

BIO 212

CHAPTER ONE

WITCHCRAFT –BELIEF, MAGICK AND SCIENCE

WITCHCRAFT - Belief, Magick and Science

Magick is real, powerful and ancient.

The power to change your life with magick is at your command. Once you understand some background and keep your intent focused, there is a very high rate of success. You do not need to have a belief in the religion to be a practitioner of their magick.

Wicca or Witchcraft is a positive religion thousands of years old. It is pre-Christian. Also known as the Old Religion, it is a religion of nature. The people who believe in this religion are called witches, both male and female. The term "warlock" is not used because it is considered to be an insult. The term warlock is equivalent to "oath breaker," or "traitor." At the time of the witch burnings, also known as the Burning Times, male Christians would infiltrate the covens. When they knew who all the witches were, they would go back to the church and turn them in. Warlock was the name given to these infiltrators who were considered traitors by the coven.

The religion is considered very personal. Typically, you will not find a Wiccan trying to convert anyone to their belief system since they respect the religions of others. It is a religion made up of both realities working together-science and magick. A Witch or Wiccan does not need to be born into the religion. It is a matter of individual choice.

This belief system is not Satanic. Satan is only a Christian concept. Witches do not have the devil as part of their religion. What they do believe in is: honor (sacredness being in all things), responsibility for our environment, love, helping, living "with" people and nature, Karma, that the life forces in nature are rhythmical and connect to the phases of the moon, reincarnation, a Supreme Being, duality(God/Goddess, Priest/Priestess, Positive/Negative, Men/Women, Black/White, Yin/Yang, etc. =Balance).

Some of what they do consist of working with agriculture, animals, wildlife, plants, ecology, psychic and magickal abilities, astrology, planetary connections, tides, healing.

CHAPTER TWO

YOUR TOOLS OF POWER

YOU ARE THE TOOL!!!

Tools are extensions of you. They enable you to shift realities to work with both the physical plane and the spiritual plane. They help you to focus and send power and energy. They help to shift from a Beta brain wave level to an Alpha state. The shift to an Alpha level, when we tune into our psychic state has been scientifically proven. Tools are really an aid.

They are symbols that the conscious and the subconscious mind utilize to gain the best results. We are all able to do this. Scientists, psychiatrists-such as Jung, practitioners and Wiccans, all tap into the same source.

The tools you can use are unlimited. Such as colors, music, dance, breath, fasting, meditation, hypnosis, scents, candles, repeating sounds-such as mantras or poetic verse, physical positions, places, symbols, ceremonies, rituals, charms and divination.

They are too numerous to name. However, there are some tools that you will need to be aware of.

BOOK OF SHADOWS — also called a grimoire. This is where you write your pells, thoughts, symbols, dreams and any other secrets. In Wiccan tradition, upon the death of a witch, this book was passed down within the family. If there weren't any surviving members of the family or anyone continuing the Wiccan tradition, then the book was burned. In our time, this practice depends on each individual Wiccan. What he/she wants to be done.

CANDLES- has varied uses. Symbolizes fire and Light. Higher knowledge. The color of the candle can heighten your intent. Make sure you do not use a color that conflicts with your purpose.

INCENSE and BURNER - element of air. Protection. Varied uses.

SALT- protection and purification.

SWORD - element of air. Used for protection, to make the circles, to send energy for a purpose.

POWDERS - the vibrations enhance your work.

HERBS, FLOWERS and TREES - they work with or without your belief being put into them. They are living and have their own vibrational energies. They can be utilized in such areas as healing, purification, divination and spells.

GEMS and STONES - since they have some of the same elements in their structure as the physical body, they are compatible. Among their versatile uses, they accelerate the wearer's psychic abilities, as well as healing, meditation and stability.

CHARMS - these can be amulets or talisman. This is an object consecrated by sending psychic force into it, thereby bringing specific changes to its owner.

ALTAR - an honored physical object or place utilized as a focus point. You can heighten or change your consciousness here. A place to set up your spiritual work. The more frequently you use the same spot, the stronger the energy will become over time.

ATHAME - this is a 2 edged knife used in magickal workings. Usually steel` or iron. Utilized to direct energy for a purpose. Or to cut staffs, rods, wands and other wood. The two edges symbolize balance.

WAND, STAFF and ROD - wood staffs of various lengths. Some types of Wood for their magickal use would be willow, peach, hazel, ash, oak, cherry and apple.

CAULDRON - used for brewing, cooking and magick. A sacred object. It represents creation. Connected to the water element and the Goddess.

CHALICE - a cup with the same meaning as the cauldron. Can hold water or meade (wine).

BELL - vibrational energy. Make sure you like the sound when it is rung. Changes the vibration of the area. Used for invocations, for protection and ritual work.

PENTACLE - usually on a flat rock, wood, clay, or other material with symbols on it. Used for protection, but can also be utilized to evoke spirits.

MORTAR and PESTLE - or a small dish. Good for making herbs into powder or mixing them. Here ingredients can be added together.

CORD - can be worn, used to make a circle and for knot magick.

PENTAGRAM - the symbol is a five-pointed star. Connected to the element of earth. Represents man. Standing up with arms and legs stretched out to the side, head at the top. It can be used as a base for ceremonies. Works as a shield of protection. Passive and defensive.

BOLLINE - a curved knife with a white handle. Very practical in use. Such as cutting or inscribe symbols, names or whatever the situation calls for.

ROBE - you can wear one or not. Wear what makes you feel comfortable.

CONJURE BAG-some other names are gris-gris bag, mojo bag and medicine bag. You put the ingredients you need for your intent into it. You can wear it, carry it or place it somewhere for a specific purpose. They come in various colors. Use the color matching your intent. You can also make these pouches.

Part of your tools include looking at charts (such as for reference), checking the seasons, solar and lunar phases, hours, knowing symbols, colors, deciding what your true intent is, anything that you feel will help you in your venture to get the best results.

Emotions are just as important. It helps you to keep focused on your intent. You do not want to be stressed when you work. You can bring peace and harmony before you begin by various methods.

You can use oils, herbs or incense for a calming scent (as an example lavender), meditate to calm yourself and to go within, you can also do fasting. Use your altered state of alpha.

Put emotional force and expectation behind your intent.

Use the tools you are comfortable with. The ones that feel right to you or none at all. It is all up to you.

You may make different choices with each new situation. You may decide to develop a ritual that works for you. Try different formulae and see which fits you the best. What does not feel right at this time may be great in a year or two.

Experiment and Enjoy!!!

CHAPTER THREE

SYMBOLISM AND CHARTS OF THE MAGICKAL WORLD

In magick, you are IN tune with nature and are a part of it. Not separated from it. Wiccans and practitioners are aware of the conscious and the unconscious workings of the mind. Aware of nature and how it moves in a cyclical form. The colors and scents around us and the responses they evoke. Sometimes without us being aware that we are reacting to them.

We all react to symbols. Even when we do not think about it or question it. It is still there and bringing out a response from you. Emotional, mental, spiritual or physical. Much as we do not think about our breathing, our heartbeat or the blood flows through our veins, they all work automatically.

Take a moment and think of the following: a cross, a pentagram, and the color red. What did you think? What did you feel? As an example: everyone has a response to red. If you are driving a car, you will stop at a red light. It is expected. Yet, if you are running through the jungle and see a red light, you would still look and stop. Even if it is only for a few seconds. The response is automatic. The reaction to this color is one of the reasons it is consciously chosen for the traffic light. It is also known that using a red rug in a room will make you stay longer in the room. You will notice that many restaurants will use the color if they want you to stay (and eat) longer. Fast food places tend to use colors such as orange. This `makes you feel energetic and gets you in and out faster. Thus, they have more of a turn over.

In the past, people counted on the knowledge of natural cycles to survive. Much as the animal kingdom does. Knowledge of what the cycle of the seasonal changes was. What the moon and sun cycles were.

Knowing when winter would come again gave people time to hunt and store food in time. Otherwise, many would not have survived the cold, barren winter months.

The Solistice and Equinox would mark the beginning of the seasons.

Their survival depended upon their need and ability to plan ahead,

Over time, all people developed their own systems of keeping track of what worked consistently. They incorporated this knowledge into religions, folk lore or whatever means helped them to remember. Situations such as burning candles or tracking the movements of the stars for knowledge of the seasons or to find the way home were survival issues.

Your own psychic and magickal power always outweighs everything else. It always comes first.

The following charts and symbols will help you to add more force or power behind your magick. Use them when you want that extra boost or as a part of your rituals or work to automatically heighten them. Much of the information has been around for an untold amount of years. Remember, if they did not work, they would not have been repeated and passed down as successful.

Make up your own spells and refer to the charts and symbols as a reference point when you need to.

The power is within you. Yet, we are also all connected to nature. It is a very real part of us. These charts and symbols will put you into the flow of nature's energies. Thus, you can work with nature, not against its natural course.

Remember, if you respond consciously to outside forces, you can work with them to bring positive manifestations into your life. You can also use them in a positive way on others to bring results that you want.

Work toward your highest potential. All of us on the planet are continually going through transformation. That is a natural part of our development. Use the esoteric knowledge to grow and improve your life, as well as that of others. Be open to the creative energies. You are meant to be happy. To accomplish goals. To celebrate life in yourself and in everything. Allow yourself to be powerful, happy, healthy and use your knowledge to let yourself be unlimited by anyone or anything. Let yourself be free.

CHARTS AND SYMBOLS

TABLE OF PLANETARY HOURS

	HOURS OF THE DAY	SUN	MON.	TUES.	WED.	THURS	FRI.	SAT.
SUNRISE	1ST	SUN	MOON	MARS	MERCURY	JUPITER	VENUS	SATURN
	2ND	VENUS	SATURN	SUN	MOON	MARS	MERCURY	JUPITER
	3RD	MERCURY	JUPITER	VENUS	SATURN	SUN	MOON	MARS
	4TH	MOON	MARS	MERCURY	JUPITER	VENUS	SATURN	SUN
	5TH	SATURN	SUN	MOON	MARS	MERCURY	JUPITER	VENUS
MIDDAY	6TH	JUPITER	VENUS	SATURN	SUN	MOON	MARS	MERCURY
	7TH	MARS	MERCURY	JUPITER	VENUS	SATURN	SUN	MOON
	8TH	SUN	MOON	MARS	MERCURY	JUPITER	VENUS	SATURN
	9TH	VENUS	SATURN	SUN	MOON	MARS	MERCURY	JUPITER
	10TH	MERCURY	JUPITER	VENUS	SATURN	SUN	MOON	MARS
	11TH	MOON	MARS	MERCURY	JUPITER	VENUS	SATURN	SUN
EVENING	12TH	SATURN	SUN	MOON	MARS	MERCURY	JUPITER	VENUS
	HOUR OF THE NIGHT							
SUNSET	1ST	JUPITER	VENUS	SATURN	SUN	MOON	MARS	MERCURY
TWILIGHT	2ND	MARS	MERCURY	JUPITER	VENUS	SATURN	SUN	MOON
NIGHTFALL	3RD	SUN	MOON	MARS	MERCURY	JUPITER	VENUS	SATURN
	4TH	VENUS	SATURN	SUN	MOON	MARS	MERCURY	JUPITER
	5TH	MERCURY	JUPITER	VENUS	SATURN	SUN	MOON	MARS
MIDNIGHT	6TH	MOON	MARS	MERCURY	JUPITER	VENUS	SATURN	SUN
	7TH	SATURN	SUN	MOON	MARS	MERCURY	JUPITER	VENUS
	8TH	JUPITER	VENUS	SATURN	SUN	MOON	MARS	MERCURY
	9TH	MARS	MERCURY	JUPITER	VENUS	SATURN	SUN	MOON
	10TH	SUN	MOON	MARS	MERCURY	JUPITER	VENUS	SATURN
	11TH	VENUS	SATURN	SUN	MOON	MARS	MERCURY	JUPITER
	12TH	MERCURY	JUPITER	VENUS	SATURN	SUN	MOON	MARS

SYMBOLS FOR THE FIVE ELEMENTS

$\triangle$ = Fire

∇ = Water

$\ominus$ = Earth

$\oslash$ = Air

$\bigcirc$ = Spirit

ELEMENT CORRESPONDENCES

Element	Direction	Color	Season	Sun Location
Air	East	Yellow Gold White Light blue	Spring	Rise
Earth	North	Black Green Gold Purple	World between lives Winter	Invisible world
Fire	South	Red Gold Orange	Maturity Summer	Highest point
Water	West	Blue Black Silver	Fall Decline	Sets

CONTINUED-CORRESPONDENCES

Element	Tarot Card	Tool	Sense	Energies
Air	Ace of Swords	Sword	Hearing	Mind
Earth	Ace of Pentacles	Shield	Touch	Heart
Fire	Ace of Rods	Rod	Smell	Physical Body
Water	Ace of Cups	Cup	Taste	Spirit

You have numerous tools at your disposal. The following are meant as examples. Do not limit yourself.

VARIOUS TOOLS

Element	Tools
Air	Incense, Feather, Wind Chimes, Breezes
Earth	Dish or bowl with salt, Gems, Stones
Fire	Candle, Athame, Volcanic Ash or Stone
Water	Trident, Chalice, Bowl, Cauldron

PURPOSE

Utilize the following correlations when working magick.

Air: Psychic abilities, Thoughts, Inspiration, Ideas, Creativity, Illuminators, The Hierophant, Main control, Initiatory Rites, Power behind the Veil, Inner plane order, Brain stimulation, Oriental mind fullness, Awareness, Philosophies, Communication, Meditation, Focus, Perception, Knowledge abstracted from Chaos, Organization from disorganization, Awakening high Intellect.

Earth: Prosperity, Money, Growth, Success, Business, Employment, Wisdom, Connectors, Truth, Rituals, Symbol interpretation, Applied and Theoretical Magick, Measuring and planning work, Teaching, Learning, Codes (Ex: DNA), Authority, Responsibility, Deep levels in Pathworking, Nature philosophy, Feelings, Possessions, Practicality, Patience.

Fire: Action, Passion, Change, How you see situations, Transmutation, Faith, Protectors, Courage, Love, Self-healing, Rest, Renewal, Relationships, Western Philosophy, Vulnerability, Self- purification, Strength, Will, Drive, Humor, Cleverness, Knowledge of environment.

Water: Love, Marriage, Healing, Emotions, Relationships, Sacred dreams, Dream work, Initiators, Journeys, Deep psychic work, Communication with spirit guides, Deep meditation, Introspection, Hibernation, Inner self-knowledge, Eastern spiritual philosophy, Intuition, Akashic Records, Astral plane, Astral fluids.

CORRESPONDENCE of MAGICK and ASTROLOGY

Sunday	Ruled by the Sun
Monday	Ruled by the Moon
Tuesday	Ruled by Mars
Wednesday	Ruled by Mercury
Thursday	Ruled by Jupiter
Friday	Ruled by Venus
Saturday	Ruled by Saturn

PLANETARY ACTIVITIES

SUN: Gaining favor; friends; wealth; healing; good fortune; operations concerning employers; promotions.

MOON: Love; messages; travel; emotions; medicine; dreams.

MERCURY: Study; fast luck; quick money; business; divination; Spiritual work; to lift hexes.

VENUS: Making friends; travel; love; fertility; art.

MARS: Energy; passion; war (offense and defense).

JUPITER: Preserving health; gaining riches; obtaining honors; legalities; court success.

SATURN: Causing good or bad fortune to business; learning; destruction; gaining possessions; Spiritual work for protection; legalities for family; lift negativity and protect from enemies.

ASTROLOGY and ALCHEMY

Planet	Symbol	Metal	Colors
Sun	☉	Gold	Gold, Yellow
Jupiter	♃	Tin	Blue
Mars	♂	Iron	Red
Venus	♀	Copper	Green
Mercury	☿	Quicksilver	Gray, Neutral
Saturn	♄	Lead	Black
Moon	☽	Silver	White, Silver

CHAKRAS AND COLORS

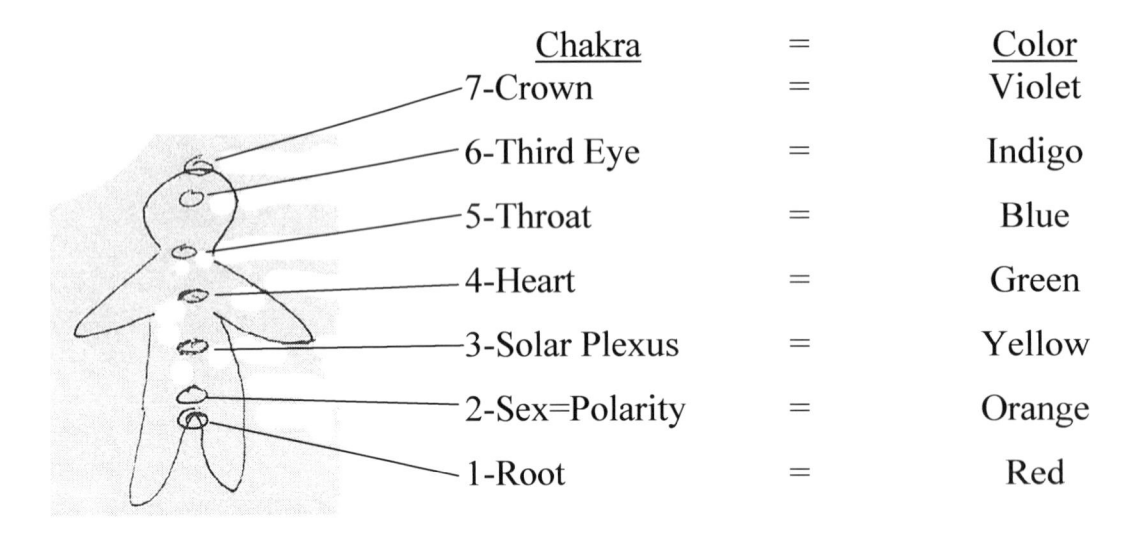

Chakra	=	Color
7-Crown	=	Violet
6-Third Eye	=	Indigo
5-Throat	=	Blue
4-Heart	=	Green
3-Solar Plexus	=	Yellow
2-Sex=Polarity	=	Orange
1-Root	=	Red

There are more chakras. We work with 16. However for our purpose here, the accepted 7 is good for magickal use.

COLORS

Use with altar cloth, candle, oil. Anything that calls for color or it can be added.

RED — Color of life; will power. Burned for love; sex appeal; sexuality; courage; health; strength; increasing energy levels. Attracts woman.

PINK — Color of affection and service; truthfulness. Burned for love; honor; gentleness and Spiritual awakening; diplomacy; success; health.

RED & PINK — Attract men.

ORANGE — Color of joy and enthusiasm; prosperity; energy; courage; adaptability. Burned to influence friendships; stimulation; increase mental strength.

YELLOW — Color of intellect and imagination; invokes spirits; creative; action; cheerfulness; joy; warmth and strength.

BLUE — Color of balance and abundance. Burned for stability; youthfulness; attracts money; success; luck; healing; fertility; good crops; health; cooperation and generosity.

BROWN — Color of practicality and solidarity; earthly planes; legal and material levels. Burned for slowing down mental process; balance; thrift; telepathic communication.

BLACK — Color of negativity and depression; un-hexing. Burned for banishing rituals; remembrance and mourning; protection from evil; shield.

VIOLET — Color of sentimentality and royalty. Burned for tranquility and sedation.

PURPLE — Color of luxury and power. Burned for ambition; wisdom; psychic development; draws in spiritual energy; protection; self esteem; goal attainment; prestige and spirit contact. (Recommended burning a white candle also).

SILVER — Color of stability, neutrality. Burned for psychic development; remove evil influence; good conquering evil.

GOLD — Color of universal brotherhood. Burned for good health; good fortune; intellect; teaching; persuasive; universal love.

ELEMENT-BODY- COLOR CORRESPONDENCES

Element	Body	Color
Fire	Head	Red
Air	Chest	Yellow
Water	Abdominal	Blue
Earth	The rest of the body below abdominal	Brown

COLORS AND MUSIC

Violet = Musical note "B"

Indigo = Musical note "A"

Blue = Musical note "G"

Green = Musical note "F"

Yellow = Musical note "E"

Orange = Musical note "D"

Red = Musical note "C"

THE WITCHES' SABBATS

IMBOLC - also known by the names: Lady Day, Candlemas, Oimelc. Celebrated on February 2nd.

SPRING EQUINOX - also called Festival of the Trees, Alban Eilir, Vernal Equinox, Rite of Eostre, Ostara. Celebrated in March, when the night and the day are equal in length. There are other dates given for this day. However,, this timing seems most accurate.

BELTANE - also called May Day, Rudemas, Walpurgisnacht, Roodmass. Held on April 30th at night or May 1st. Some dates claim May 5th. I suggest May 1st.

SUMMER SOLSTICE - also called Midsummer, Alban HEFIN, Litha. Celebrated on the first day of summer. Longest day of the year.

LAMMAS - also known as August Eve, Lughnasadh, First Festival of Harvest, Lady Day Eve. Celebrated on the eve of July 31st. Some celebrate August 1st.

AUTUMN EQUINOX - also called the Fall Sabbat, Alban Elfred, Second Festival of Harvest, Mabon. Celebrated on the first day of Fall.

SAMHAIN- also called All Hallows' Eve, All Saints' Eve, and the Third Festival of Harvest, Festival of the Dead, Shadowfest, Hallowmas. Held on November 7th. Some hold it on October 1st. It is still debated.

YULE - also called Winter Solstice, Alban Arthan, Winter Rite, and Midwinter. Held on the first day of winter or December 22nd.

The dates, in which there are various changes, are due to the fact that there are numerous traditions. Depending on which tradition you utilize, the dates will vary.

Many Sabbats are celebrated starting at night and the following day.

They are considered solar holidays.

WHEEL OF THE YEAR

A full cycle of the year. It starts at Samhain. The symbol is an eight-spoked wheel. Representing the seasons and the sun. The wheel represents the cycle of birth, death-rebirth. The wheel turns with the seasons.

SOME BASIC HOLIDAY MEANINGS

IMBOLC - banishing the winter season. Changing from the old to the new. Celebrates spring coming in. New beginnings.

SPRING EQUINOX - celebrates the fertility of spring and of the earth.

BELTANE - fertility and love are celebrated. All forms of fertility are included. Such as the growth of crops or of ideas.

SUMMER SOLSTICE - good for harvesting herbs, healing rituals, divination, all magick, dream work, working with the earth, forests and magickal beings.

LAMMAS - give thanks for the harvests. Harvesting herbs for magickal purposes.

AUTUMN EQUINOX - giving thanks, meditation, going within yourself to gain perspective.

SAMHAIN - the veil between the two realities is at the weakest point of the year. Good to call in spirits, to communicate with the other side, divination.

YULE - celebrates the sun's rebirth, the past years success, love and family.

ESBATS

A time to do magickal workings.

The Esbats are the days and nights. They are Full Moon and New Moon times.

<u>New moon</u> - is used for new starts, new beginnings, growth, expansion, healing.

<u>Waxing moon</u> - is used for bringing or attracting magick. This is the time between the New Moon to the Waxing moon.

<u>Full moon</u> - is worked for banishing, sending negativity away, protection, divination, canceling out the things you no longer want in your life, diminishing.

<u>Waning moon</u> - is best for banishing, getting rid of negative habits, situations or people (from bothering you), ill health. Time between the Full and the New moon.

<u>Dark moon</u> - considered being three days before the New Moon.

There are thirteen Full Moons during each year.

You need to remember that even though these are highly charged times, you can work other magick. When you need to work, you need to work. These energies are meant to enhance your magick, not to limit it.

GODDESS CORRESPONDENCES

<u>Triple Goddess</u> - maiden - symbolizes waxing moon
mother - symbolizes full moon
crone - symbolizes waning moon

<u>Connections</u> - Light half of the year, silver, love, pearl, emerald, cauldron, cup, 5 pettaled flowers, mirror, seashell, earth, sea, moon, death, emotions, fertility, wisdom, moon, beauty

HORNED GOD-CORRESPONDENCES

<u>CONNECTIONS</u>: Dark half of the year, sun, gold, yellow, horns, sword, yellow, horns, sword, spear, knife, arrow, wand, forests, male sexuality, Lord of Death, Life, Underworld, wild animals, the hunt, horns symbolize the crescent moon and the forest.

THE SEVEN DIRECTIONS

East, South, West, North, Above, Below, Center.

ANKH

An ancient Egyptian symbol for life, birth, sex, fertility, health, psychic ability, communication, cosmic wisdom, rebirth

PENTAGRAM

1. represents the element of water
2. represents the element of fire
3. represents the element of metal
4. represents the element of wood
5. represents the element of earth

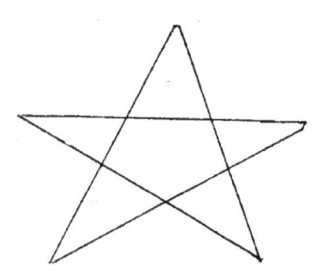

PENTAGRAM TALISMAN

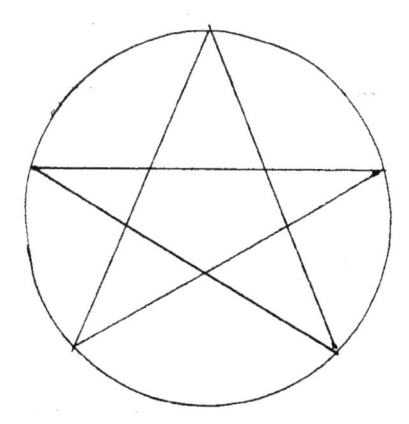

Very ancient and powerful symbol. Make in silver or on parchment paper. Represents perfected man.

CHARMS

Symbols for the Spirit of the planet. You can draw it on parchment paper and use black ink.

STAR OF DAVID

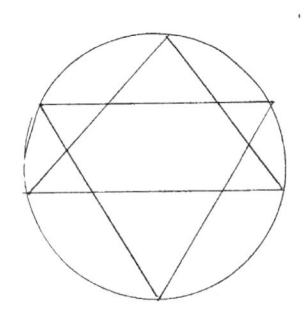

Symbolizes man's ascension into spirit and descent into matter. Common connection " As above, so below".

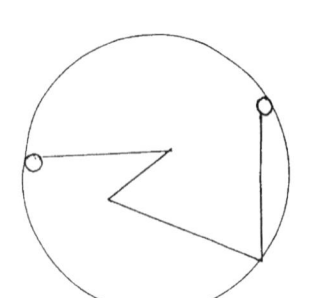

SUN

Symbolizes life force, wisdom, will, the heart, power.

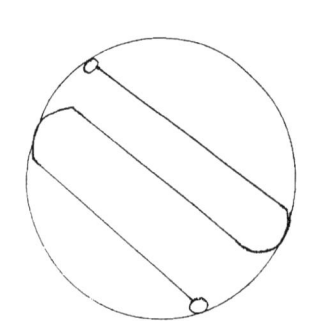

SATURN

Symbolizes purification, stabilizing force. Rules magickal and religious ceremonies.

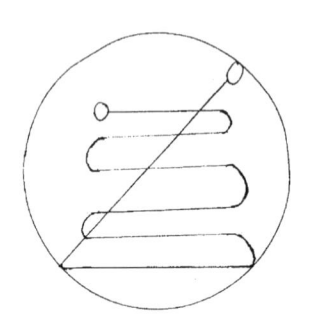

MOON

Symbolizes intuition, emotion and imagination.

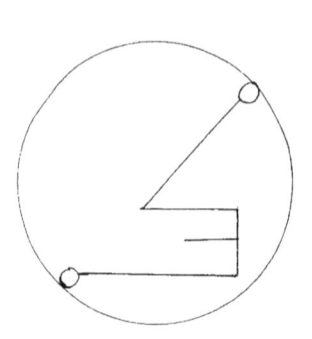

VENUS

Symbolizes love, emotions, marriage, friendship, unity.

JUPITER

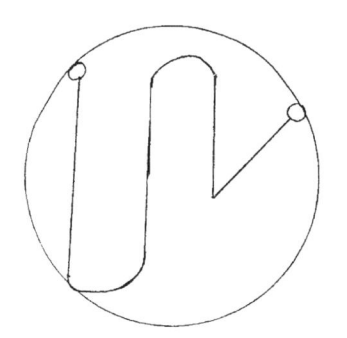

Symbolizes fortune, expansion, individual growth, wealth.

KEY OF SOLOMON

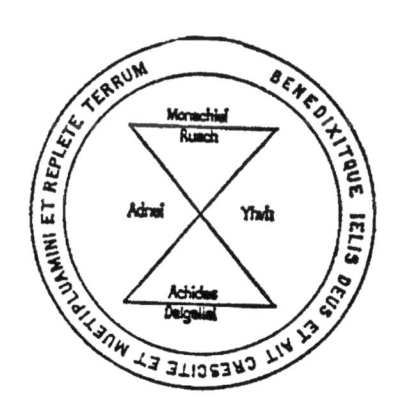

Talisman for love. Releasing psychic energy.

SEAL OF AGRIPPA

Utilized to attract success in attracting positive magickal and material outcomes.
Protects against evil.

BUSINESS SUCCESS

Amulet for success in business.

SUCCESS

Said to gain wealth, success and to bring a long life.

TRISKELION

Varied versions.
Symbolizes motion, progress, moving ahead.
Religious balance (symbolic of the Number 3)

SYMBOLS AND USES

△ = Triangle. Energizes. Activating force.

○ = Circle. Protection. Positive force. Good for meditation, dreamwork, pathwork.

△ = Pyramid. Heightening force. Increases ability, longevity. An amplifier.

△▽ = Fire and water. 2 opposites. Warm and cold=red and white=soul and body=sun and moon=man and woman.

☉ = Sun, God, Belief, Union, Eternal Light.

▭ = Rectangle. Represents the terrestrial world.

☥ = Crux Ansata. Healing

⊤ = Tau, Fertility.

+ = Equal armed cross. Balance.

⚹ = Wealth Finances. Money in business.

)O(= Goddess.

☽ = New Beginnings, Motherhood, Feminine Energy.

☉ = The God.

🌀 = Spiral, Movement upward, Growth.

✡ = Seal of Solomon. Represents human soul. Used in all forms of magick. Purifies. Wisdom. Psychic ability.

ALCHEMY

Fire   -   electric energy

Water -   magnetic energy

Air   -   neutral energy

Earth -   grounding energy

CORRESPONDENCE CHART

EAST

Air

Yellow, White, Gold, Light Blue

God	Goddess
Ra	Diana
Dionysus	Kwan Yin
Hermes	Eosphorus
Mercury	Venus
Thoth	Aphrodite
Jupiter	Hecate
Thor	Freya

WEST

Water

Blue, Black, Silver

God	Goddess
Neptune	Selena
Poseidon	Anu
Njord	Selene

NORTH

Earth

Black, Green, Gold, Purple

God	Goddess
Hapi	Athena
Dionysus	Minerva
	Coatlicue

SOUTH

Fire

Red, Gold, Orange

God	Goddess
Vishnu	Danu
Woden	Bridget
Pele	Mary

SEAL OF THE SUN

CHAPTER FOUR

PROTECTION AND BLESSINGS – YOUR UNSEEN FORCES

Protection is a very powerful force. You can protect yourself as well as others or objects. It is very important in any undertaking to establish first that you are safe. There are various methods, so pick one or more that you feel fits the situation best. Once you are safe, you can feel at ease about working magick. If you inadvertently make a mistake, it will not matter. Use it prior to all psychic and magickal work.

Protection in all forms has been utilized for centuries. As verbal spells, in visualizations, talisman, herbal blends oils and dolls, to name a few.

You can use the invocation at the beginning of this book to help you get started.

Always focus on what your intent is, otherwise you will tone down its power.

Blessings are very common and are with us and around us in our everyday lives. We no longer notice or think of them in a way that would give them more power. Nonetheless, they are still in use. As an example, when someone sneezes, you say "God Bless You" or "Bless You". You will hear the term "Praise Be" or 'Thank God' and never think twice.

Learn to use it consciously and with focused intent to put meaning and power behind it.

A CHILDS' PROTECTION PRAYER/SPELL

Good to say prior to sleep, when in danger or at any other time.
Repeat 3 times at times of danger.

> Bridget, Goddess of the a fire,
>
> Surround me with your protective Light,
>
> Let nothing negative or harmful,
>
> Come within this circle of fire.
>
>
> So Mote It Be.

BLESSING FOR A CHILD

Hold your hand, Palm down, either hand or both, over the top of a childs' head. This is above the Crown Chakra. If you are not physically able to do this, such as being in a distant location, use a picture of the child. Hold your hand in the same position.

Focus on White Light coming down through the top of your head (Crown Chakra), out through your palm and into the child.

Next, repeat the following words with intent.

> Triple Goddess,
>
> I invoke thee,
>
> Bless this child (or insert the Childs' name),
>
> With your might.
>
>
> Through the power of the Lady,
>
> Bless this child (or use the name),
>
> With Love and Light.
>
>
> So Mote It Be.

CIRCLE OF SELF-PROTECTION

Visualize yourself standing in the center of White Light. If you can not 'see" it, just know that it is there. "See " or "know" the light is spinning all around you from your left towards your right clockwise. As it spins, it surrounds you 100%, as well as above your head and below your feet. As it spins, it is so fast that it seems like a solid wall (ceiling and floor).

Focus your mind on how long you want it there for protection. Then state: This circle of protection surrounds me completely for (a day, etc.).

Next, relax and walk away. It will be around you until the time you set it up for.

You can also time it-until <u>what the situation is</u> (state what it is exactly as possible) comes to a conclusion (or completion).

Circle represents molecules

Atom represents us

Nucleus represents our brain

HOME PROTECTION AND BLESSING

Take some Patchouly Oil and place a drop or two in the palms of your hands. Rub your palms together lightly.

Mix the following herbs together:

Ash, broom, some grass, sage, rose

Put a few drops of the Patchouly Oil on the blended herbs.

Walk to all for corners of your home. If you have an apartment, it is not in each individual room, but the Four Corners of the apartment. If you live in a house, it is the Four Corners of each floor. Including the basement.

Start at the eastern corner until you come back to it again. (You will do the East corner twice).

Walk to each corner and sprinkle a little of the herbal blend there. As you do this, say with intent: "Three times in each corner".

Odin, of the Northern Lights,

    Goddess, Bless this entire house.

Bless it with peace and harmony,
Fill it with abundance and charity.

Let the love flow in,
Let it surround this house.

Bless all who live here,
Protect it all around.

May all those who enter here,
Blessed Be, Blesses Be.

Visualize the White Light as a protective walls from corner to corner, floor to ceiling.

BLESSING UPON A JOB

The happier you are at what you do, the better it will go. Which in turn will make you happy. An all around positive cycle.

Stand with your legs shoulder width apart. Your arms stretching toward the sky above your head. Your head leaning back as if looking up at the sky. Close your eyes.

Stand in this position for a minute. You might feel a tingling sensation in your fingers. You are gathering energy.

Next, say aloud, with focused intent:

I call in Osiris and Thor.

I invoke Mercury.

I call in Fortuna and Brigid.

Bless me with protection and prosperity,

So that I can do my best,

Bless me with a quick and just mind,

To help with people and my job,

Bless me that fortune smile on me,

To heighten my skills and protective shields.

Bless me with wisdom,

To do my best,

Bless my job with happiness.

So Mote It Be.

DOLL OF PROTECTION - For House

Take a white cloth and cut 2 pieces to look like a doll.

Sew around the sides and bottom. Leave a small opening at the top to fill with the following:

- 1 turquoise stone
- 1 apache tear stone
- 1/3 violet-flower
- 1/3 rosemary-herb
- 1/3 geranium-flower

Sew the top closed. Hold the doll between your palms. Focus your intent and say:

> Through the God and Goddess, this doll will now protect this house from all evil and negativity.

Then put the doll somewhere facing your front door. It does not have to be visual. You can place it under a chair, with your flower pot (decorative), make it very small to fit in a small spot, etc.

Once every six months hold it in your hands and repeat the verbal part of the spell. This will reactivate it.

THE ALTAR OF PROTECTION RITUAL

Set your altar so it faces East.
Place a violet cloth on it. Then place a white cloth over it so both colors show.
Set up your altar as drawn below:

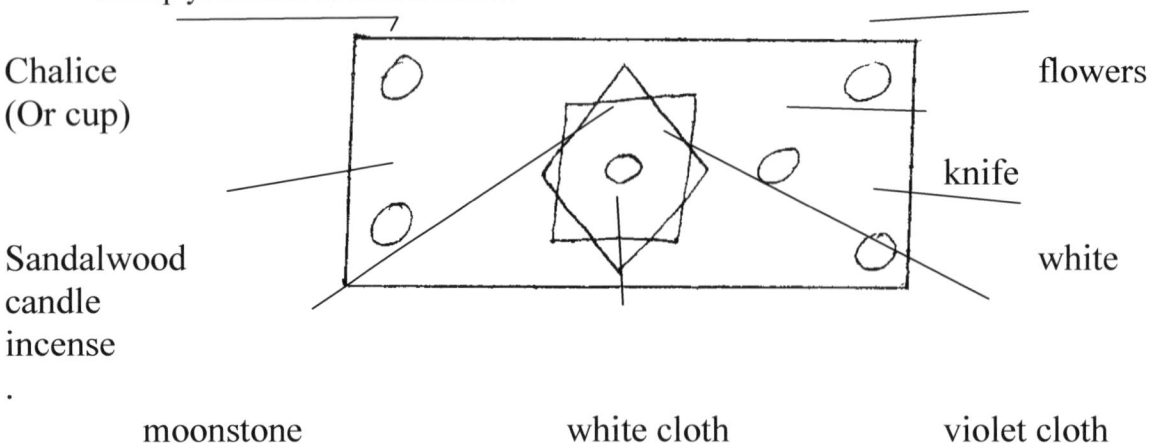

Chalice (Or cup)

flowers

knife

Sandalwood candle incense

white

moonstone   white cloth   violet cloth

1. Light the candle.

2. Pick up the chalice and say- I call on you Great Lady to protect me in all my endeavors.

   Give me your Blessing. -

   Place the chalice back.

3. Pick up the incense and say: I call on you Lord of the Hunt to protect me in all my endeavors.

   Give me your Blessing.

   Put it back

4. Pick up the flowers, holding them in front of you, wave them over the altar from left to right, saying: In the name of the Great Lady, in cleanse this place and make it sacred. Bless the altar and the work done with it.

   Place it back.

5. Pick up the knife and aim the point toward the stone and say: In the name of the Lord of the Hunt, I send all the protective forces into this stone. (Visualize the energy flowing through your arms, into the knife, then into the stone). This stone of protection is now active.

Put the knife back.

6. Say-Thank you Great Lady and Lord of the Hunt. Blessed Be.
7. Walk away. Leave the candle lit. When the flame goes out, pick up the stone and carry it with you at all times (within three feet of your body), or place it in a spot where you need protective energy.

In doing this ritual with others, one person can do everything (as the solitary witch does) or one person can pick up each object while others take turns with the verbal part. If you do this ritual in a group, you can place several stones in the center. One for each person.

PROTECTION BATH

In a small muslin pouch add the following ingredients:

Violet and Lavender flowers
A pinch of sea salt.

Tie the pouch with three knots.

In a bathtub, place it under hot running water. When the tub starts filling up, add some cold water until it reaches a comfortable warm level. Soak in it for 15-20 minutes. Do not use soap at this time or shampoo. This would change the vibration of the water.

SWORD OF PROTECTION

You can use a sword or a wood or copper staff.

Do this outdoors for full effect. If you can not, make sure you clear a spot to make room first in your work area.

Stand with the sword in your power hand (the one you write with). Focus on White Light or Golden-White Light coming from above your head, down through the top of your head (Crown Chakra), and into the sword. The sword is an extension of your body, not something you just hold.

Point the sword away from you, touching the ground, with your arm extended. Slowly draw a circle in the dirt or visualize the circle. As you move clockwise, "see" White Light coming out of the tip and drawing a circle of Light. Make sure you do not break contact with the ground and that you end the circle connecting it to the start. If you break the contact, start over again.

As you draw your circle with yourself in the center, verbally or mentally <u>say</u>-

Through the Goddess and God I consecrate the circle with Power, Protection

And Light. Nothing negative or harmful can get in. And as I will, so note it be.

When you finished your circle stand in the middle with the sword held high, pointing toward the sky. <u>Say</u> -

> Oh great Goddess and God,
>
> I celebrate all life with you.
>
> You are the earth and the sky,
>
> The yin and the yang,
>
> The Light and the Dark.
>
> Through you flows all creation.
>
> Protect me in (<u>fill in with the time or situation :</u>
>
> <u>Ex: my travels),</u>
>
> Protect me!
>
> Protect me!
>
> Protect me!

Then point your sword tip down to touch the ground where the circle ended. Touching the circle, go in the opposite direction and visualize the circle disappearing as your sword passes over its lines.

A BLESSING CIRCLE RITUAL

Hold the following stones in your hand: an amethyst, obsidian, jade and a tiger's eye.

When you want to Bless an object, to carry with you as an example. Or to Bless an other person or yourself, then you would use this ritual

Place the object on a flat surface. You can either use a picture of yourself or a friend or stand in enough space to place the stones around you.

Place the stones around the object in a clockwise direction, starting at the Eastern point. Place them in the order, they were given. <u>Repeat:</u>

> Goddess Mother of Love,
>
> Bless (<u>the object or person</u>),
>
> You of the hearth and home,
>
> Of the water and flowers,
>
> The creative force.
>
> Bless (<u>the object or person</u>).
>
> Air and Fire,
>
> Water and Earth,
>
> Bless (<u>the object or person</u>)
>
> Through the power of the Goddess Mother.
>
> Blessed Be.

Then pick up the stones in reverse order. You can save them in a pouch if you would like, to use further at an other time.

Use for blessing purposes.

ELIXIR OF THE EARTHLY FORCE

Get a stone called turquoise. Wash it well. Place it in a chalice or cup that is made of glass. Add enough water to fill it.

Place this in direct sunlight. Leave it there for one or three days.

Drink this elixir whenever you need protective energy.

You can put the water in a different container when you are finished. This way, you can store it in your refrigerator, without the stone being in the water.

INVOCATION TO THE GODDESS

As you invoke the Goddess, hold in your power hand (the one you write with) the stone that is called a clear quartz crystal.

The size and shape of the stone does not matter. Make sure it is a size you can carry.

Hold your hand with the stone directly in front of you. Invoke the Goddess:

This crystal that I now possess,

I dedicate to you.

Bring the protective energies of the universe to it,

Fire, Air, Earth and Water,

The forces and power be within it.

As the energy passes in your name to it,

Great Goddess I now invoke your power,

Your love and your force,

Activate now, this stone of power!

So Mote It Be!

TO HAVE COMPUTERS BREAK DOWN LESS FREQUENTLY- A Protection Spell.

Place a clear quartz crystal next to your computer or on top of it. Make sure the stone is not further then three feet away. The closer, the better.

Overloading or negative energy will flow into it, rather then staying in the computer.

It changes the frequency of it breaking down. If it would normally have any problems, now the percentage of this happening will be cut to 10 %.

PROTECT YOURSELF FROM NEGATIVE COWORKERS

Prior to entering your workplace, visualize yourself surrounded by the color pink.

Next, visualize that pink expanding, until it also surrounds your coworkers. You only need to expand it to cover problem or annoying people. However, you could also expand it so it covers everyone or if you are in a room, then the whole room/office.

BLESSING TREE SPELL

On a white piece of paper, write with black ink.

Write down the situation, person or object that you want Blessed. As you write, clearly visualize what you desire.

Sprinkle some of the herb named acacia or violet over it.

Take a little dirt from the ground that is closest to the tree and sprinkle that on the paper.

Fold it up and bury it as close as possible to where the roots would be.

Ask the Green Man (another name for the God) to come and Bless your intent. You can simply ask with a definite tone of voice, or make up your own verse.

Remember when you are done, to thank the Green Man.

Then, walk away and do not look back. If you look, you will cancel out the spell. In which case, you would have to start again at the beginning.

PROTECTION CORD

You need three cords of different colors. You can also use ribbon for this.

One of white, one of gold (yellow) and one of violet.

Hold the three together at one end.

Make one knot with the three strands together as one. Say with intent:

> I now make this knot in the name of the Triple Goddess.

Make the second knot and say:

> I now make this knot in the name of Pan.

Make the third knot and say:

> I now make this knot of the protective force. Activate!
>
> Activate! Activate!

Now either carry it with you or place in the area that needs protecting.

You can also put it on your keychain

CAR SECURITY

To increase the level of protection of any vehicle, do the following.

Get a clear quartz crystal. The raw stone is the best. Place it anywhere in your car. It does not have to be visual. It works on vibrational energy. Leave it there as long as you own the car.

Next, with your arm extended, palm toward the car, Bless it and say:

> It is now protected in the name of the God and Goddess.

As you do this, walk around the car three times. Ending up where you started. Either direction is fine.

It does not completely cancel incidents, but changes the outcome. It does not always cancel in case you or someone else needed to learn something from the situation.

As an example: it would either totally avoid a problem, the car might be dented, but you would be fine, a hubcap is stolen instead of the car.

It always works.

HOUSE BLESSING RITUAL

Mix some of the herb known as sage with clove oil.

Sprinkle some on the outside of all your doors leading into your home. Sprinkle some on your windows from the inside. Also sprinkle some in the center of every room. Include the attic or basement if you are in your own house. You do not need to include it in an apartment or studio.

As you sprinkle the blend, **repeat**:

>I bless this house in the name of the Triple Goddess and God.
>
>May this house be protected.
>
>May all who enter be Blessed.
>
>Bless the house with Love, Health,
>
>>Wisdom, Harmony and Prosperity.
>
>Bless it with the Three-Fold Law.
>
>Blessed Be! Blessed Be! Blessed Be!

Any of the blends that may be left should be sprinkled on the threshold of the front door.

You can do this Blessing Ritual for others, as well as for yourself.

ELEMENTAL WATER SPELL

Go to the nearest body of water. Ocean, lake, stream or whatever is close.

Take an empty bottle with you, that have never been used.

Fill the bottle with water. Standing at the edge of the water, with one hand over the bottles' top, say:

> Undines of the deepest dark,
> Neptune with your trident bright,
> Consecrate this water for me,
> Bless it with your energies.
> And as I will, so mote it be!

Then put a cap/lid on the bottle.

Any time you need Blessing energy, use some of the water from the bottle.

It can be used for the same purposes that Holy Water is used for.

BLESSING THE PLANTS, FIELDS, CROPS

New growth in the crops, plants-for food, medicinal use or magickal was always very important for survival. The survival of the community, as well as the individual.

We still have farmers, individuals who enjoy nature and growth and people who just like flowers on their windowsills.

We bless the plants to help them grow. Incantation over the plants (or visualize them):.

> Bless this (these) plant (plants),
>
> Through Mother Earth,
>
> For fertility and growth.
>
>
> To stretch toward the sky,

To be healthy and strong,

Hearty and filled with energy flow.

Then visualize a healthy, growing plant.

PROTECTION RITUAL

On a white Seven-Day candle, carve the following symbols as you visualize your intent with your knife:

Ψ   ☆   middle

Focus on your purpose. Anoint the candle with Patchouly Oil. Put 1-2 drops of the oil on your fingers and rub it onto the candle. Start at the middle and rub up to the tip of the wick. Go back to the middle and rub to the bottom.

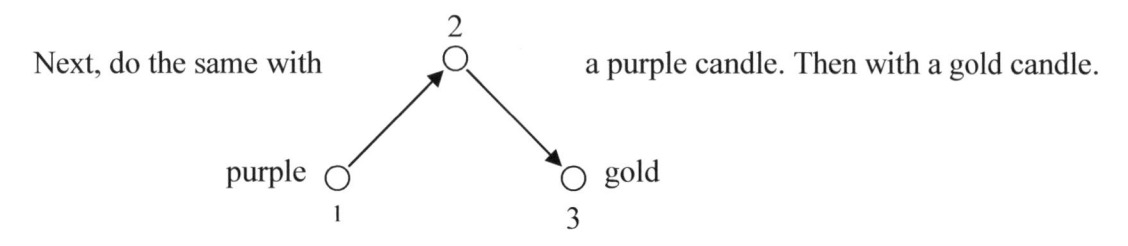

Next, do the same with a purple candle. Then with a gold candle.

Arrange these in a triangle. White at the top, purple at the left bottom point, gold at the right bottom tip.

Light them in order from 1 to 3.

Invoke with purpose:

>Great Lady of the Light,
>
>Shine on these candles,
>
>Make them bright,
>
>Protection, energy expansion,
>
>Great Lady I call on your attention.
>
>Blessed Be1
>
>Blessed Be!
>
>Blessed Be!

Let the candles burn down to their sockets. When done, if there are any wax pieces left, throw them away <u>outside</u> the house.

BLESSING PETS-ANIMALS

When survival depended on healthy dogs, cows, sheep or other animals that increased your chance of a longer life, keeping them healthy incorporated many forms. Including magickal help.

We also care about animals and pets.

We want them to be happy, as well as healthy.

Utilize a picture of your pet or the pet as a focus.

Hold your hand with the palm facing the picture.

With focus, invoke:

>Blessings upon you,
>
>Be healthy and strong,
>
>Be happy and lively,
>
>Be true to yourself.

Let the winds rise up to protect you,

Let the earth ground negative flow,

Let the fire energy activate you,

Let the water wash away your woes.

Be strong! Be healthy! Be happy!
So Mote It Be!

PINE-WIND DANCE-Protection

Gather a few twigs of pine. Three, five or seven are good numbers. Take these from a pine you selected.

Tie them together at one end with red ribbon.

Walk around the pine tree in a clockwise direction, holding the twigs. Do so three times.

Mentally think of music that has a beat. Not the words, just the music. Focus on these twigs as containing protective energy, given to you by the pine tree, by nature. Be happy and feel safe and uplifted.

As you feel the beat and focus on the purpose, allow yourself to dance to the rhythm around the tree three more times. In any movement you choose. Relax and feel the rhythm of the music, you and nature.

When you completed the last circle, thank the tree for the protection and touch it with your power hand (the one you write with). Fell the tree, the bark, anything you might be aware of with the tree. Hot, cold, etc.

Then walk away with the twigs. Wherever you put the twigs, will be the protective energy.

PROTECTIVE AMULET

On a disk shaped piece of wood, draw the following, in color:

Symbols: Odin, ⊖, ⊙, ⋈ (write your name), 7

Colors: red, white, gold, silver, black, violet

(Oil-) Start X

Example:

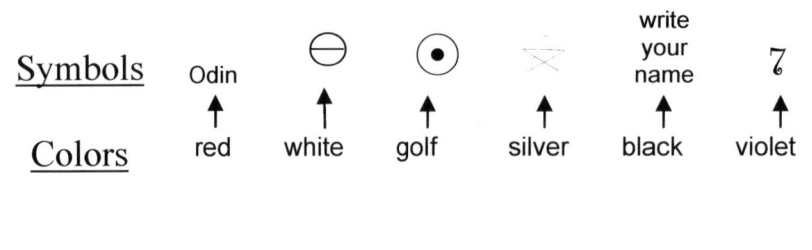

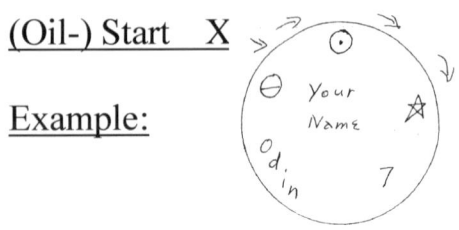

Place these symbols anywhere you feel on the disk. The best, but not limited to, woods are: oak, willow, peach, mahogany, pine. You can also use a copper or silver disk.

Next, take some Pine Oil or Patchouly Oil and put a drop or two on your finger.

Hold the disk and starting at the top left (x) of the disk, put the oil on the edge clockwise until you connect back to the start. Make sure you do not break the contact.

As you do this, focus on your intent.

When you are finished, tie a white string around it so you can suspend it in the air. Light a white candle on which you have carved the same symbols lightly. You can even use a pencil point if you do not wish to use your knife. Do not add color. Focus as you do this.

Hold the amulet by the string, just above the flame. You need to consecrate this amulet.

Focus on your intent, then say:

> By the fire of this flame,
> Flickering with Light,
> I now consecrate this amulet,
> By Odins force and might.
>
> The power has now be given,
> Three times three in fold,

Expansion of its energies,

I now in my hand hold.

Let this amulet held by me,

Consecrated it now shall be,

One hundred years of power and force,

I give this amulet that I now hold.

From dawn ' till dusk,

From dusk ' till dawn,

This amulet is one hundred strong,

As I consecrate with this force,

This amulet now has an unlimited source.

As I will, so shall it be,

From earth to sun,

From fire to sea.

So Be It.

Take the amulet from above the candle. Let the candle burn down to the bottom. Any wax left should be thrown away outdoors or outside your home.

If you are focused, this amulet should be active for the next 100 years. Carry it with you at all times. You can carry it in your wallet, pocket, purse or on your body. You can also make a hole in it before you start to enable you to wear it on a chain or cord around your neck.

When you do not carry it, you can wrap it in white material and put it away in a safe place where others will not touch it.

RUNE BINDING FOR PROTECTION

On a white pillar or 7 day candle, carve the following sigils:

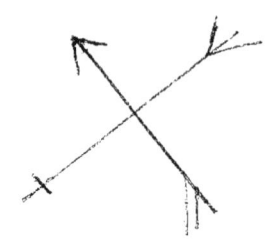

Anoint the candle from the center to the wick, then the center to the bottom, with Pine Oil.

Focus on your intent as you light it.

Sprinkle a little Rosemary and Cloves around the base.

Above the candle flame trace the Rune in the air with your right index finger. Visualize the Rune in White Light.

When you have done this, walk away. Let the candle burn down to the bottom.

Take dried wax that may be left and the herbs and put them into a white pouch. Or in the middle of a white handkerchief. Tie it together with string to close it. Tie it with 7 knots.

Carry it with you at all times. You can also place it somewhere that needs added protection. Such as your bedroom or desk at your job.

INCANTATION FOR A WATER PROTECTION SPELL

Write on a white paper, with black ink:

Neptune, Neptune of the deep,

Protect me from my enemies.

Through water that covers all the earth,

Your presence is called forth to serve.

Protect me now and ever more,

Protect me from (write down what or who or which situation   you need the protection from.)

And as I will,

So mote it be,

From sea to sky,

From sky to sea.

Now sprinkle some basil on the paper and keep a little for later.

Go to your nearest body of water. Ocean, stream, etc. Stand one foot away from the shore in the water, or three feet.

Face away from the shore holding the paper with your petition and some basil.

Open the paper and let the herb inside fly with the wind. Read (verbally or mentally) what you have written, with purpose and focus.

Fold the paper in thirds and throw it into the water away from you. Then sprinkle some of the basil you brought with you over the water and the rest throw to the wind.

Thank Neptune for his help. Turn around and walk out of the water. Do not look back.

GENERAL BLESSING

Place a cup filled with water in front of you.

Hold your hand, palm down, above the water.

Visualize White Light flowing from your palm into the water

Incant over the water:

Blessings for all,
In this water be,
To use as I want,
To bless everything.

The Triple Goddess,
In all her forms,
Bless this water,
Forever more.

Through the Goddess I can Bless,
Through this energy it manifests.

Whatever it touches,
Wherever it's sent,
The Blessings multiply,
Three times ten.

You can then put the water into a bottle for use later, or use it now.

Touch the water and sprinkle it over or near what you want Blessed.

Do this three times.

PROTECTIVE CHARM

Make or get a necklace of sandalwood. Any form is good, such as beads. Make sure there aren't any drawings on it.

Wait for a Full Moon. Then hold the necklace over some water. It can be a cup, the ocean, a stream, anything workable for you.

As you hold the necklace, chant three times:

Undines of the mystic seas,
Send protection to this tree.

At the end of the third time, add:

> Thank you Undines,
> Thank you tree,
> Blessed Be! Blessed Be!

Wear the necklace anytime you need its protection.

ANCIENT ELVES WOOD PROTECTION SPELL.

Take a piece of bark from a tree. Pine, sandalwood, oak peach, maple or willow. Stand at the roots of the tree and hold the bark in your hand. Face the tree.

Chant:

> Sylvan elves,
>
> I call you forth,
>
> Ancient fathers,
>
> Of the woods.
>
> You, who dragons remember most,
>
> You, who protect these ancient woods.
>
> Work your magick on the bark,
>
> Protection energy I now call forth.
>
> In your unending ancient realm,
>
> Deepest secrets that you command.
>
> The vast power that you hold,
>
> Send into this bark with magickal force.
>
> Protection power I now hold,

Thank you, you can now go forth.

Thank the tree for the bark and lay your palm on the trunk for a minute.

Then walk away.

You can use the bark in whatever form you need protection in. Good to add to rituals to represent earth energy.

STONE OF SAFETY DURING TRAVEL

Get a Tigers' Eye stone, A size that you can carry.

On this stone, in red ink or paint, write the following sigils:

R Y S

[When it dries, you can put nail polish or clear glaze over it to make sure it does not come off. This step is not needed].

Visualize White Light surrounding it.

Next, visualize Pink Light surrounding it. Invoke: **Gwydion.**

Gwydion, I call upon you for protection during all my travels. May this stone carry your Force, Power and Protection from now until the end of time So Mote It Be!

Do this in direct sunlight or by firelight. When you travel, carry it within three feet of you or on your body. It can be on a chain, in your pocket, wallet, pocketbook or any other convenient means.

TO WARD OFF NEGATIVE INFLUENCES IN YOUR HOME

Take a magickal knife and make the first three cuts on ash trees' limb to cut a rod. You can finish cutting it with an other tool if necessary.

Hang this above your doorway to ward off negativity.

Scatter the leaves of the ash tree in the four directions, standing in front of your home to protect the home or area.

HEX BREAKING

Blend these oils together:

    Geranium
    Bergamot
    Rue (small amount)

Wear 2-3 drops each morning. Go out with confidence, `knowing you are safe and nothing or no one can harm you.

PROTECTION FROM ILLNESS

To speed up your natural healing process and tone down the frequency of illness, carry two Tonka Beans in a green pouch around your neck.

SHIELDING

To protect your travel vehicle, use this method. You can use it on a car (bus, train, motorcycle, and plane).

Visualize the car with your energy of White Light forming a pyramid/cone shape and surround it and flowing through it.

The energy lines expand from you outward and at the same time, pull energy from above you, downward through, to within the ground and back up. It is a continuing cycle.

Once you have visualized this, it will be in effect.

You can also add a time. Such as-you want the shield up until you reach your destination.

To protect your home, visualize a dome effect from above your home to a few feet below the ground. Do this the same way you would for the car.

57

AVOID DANGER

Wear or carry a red agate stone to fend danger off. Also wards off snake bites.

PEACEFUL HOME

Burn Rose Incense.

Carry the stone called Beryl to preserve peace in your home and place a small stone in each room.

BRINGS PROTECTION AND BLESSING

Each morning when you awake, face the East. Stand with your legs spread out to the sides and your arms at shoulder level to the sides, palms down. The shape of the Pentagram!

Say-

>The East Protects!
>Send us your protection and blessings.
>Sand us Kwan Yin and Apollo.
>Send peace and harmony.
>   So Be It!

Put your arms down and go about your day.

TO STOP T.V. INTERFERENCE

Place a spider plant with a clear quartz crystal next to your T.V. If you have more then one, it should be placed next to each one.

TO CANCEL DEPRESSION

This always works. Utilized for canceling depression and magick depression.

Buy a Lapidolite stone.

Tape the stone on the inside of each forearm.

Use it constantly until you see results. Maybe longer.

PROTECTION AND HEX BREAKING

Take Tigers' Eye stone and cleanse it under running water. This can be done in a stream or under your faucet. Dry it for 3 days in direct sun light.

Place it in the center of a piece of Royal Blue material. Fold it around the stone and tie it closed with a white or Royal Blue cord. Use 3 knots.

Carry this with you at all times or until the hex is broken.

Works within seven days.

EXORCISM

Use an infusion of the roots of the plant known as Solomon's Seal. Sprinkle it around the area.

Next, light some Sage and again walk around the area.

Focus mentally on " anything or anyone negative leaves NOW, through Divine Power and Force".

Keep repeating this from start to finish.

SEND AWAY EVIL

For protection, place some branches from a Plum tree over your doors and windows. It keeps evil out.

HOUSE PROTECTION

Plant Lilac near your home to protect it and to drive away evil energies.

GOURDS FOR PROTECTION

On Samhain, the faces were cut out and placed in front of your door to scare away evil spirits.

Carry pieces of a Gourd in your pocket or pocketbook to protect yourself against evil.

A Gourd was often made into a rattle after being dried. When it made a rattling sound, it is said it drives away evil spirits.

HOUSE BLESSING KIT

You will need:

    Florida water

    Sage

    High John Incense

    Blesssing Oil

    House Blessing Soap

    2-white candles

Take some of the Florida Water and sprinkle some in each room. As you do so, in each room ask for the Blessing of Divine Power for your home and the people who occupy it. Then take sage and go to each room and with the sage lit, walk in a clockwise circle around the room, until you come back to your starting point. When all the rooms are done, put the Sage out so it does not burn. (You can put it out in sand if you would like for earth energy grounding).

Next, light High John Incense in your bedroom and let it burn out by itself.

Take a few drops of Blessing Oil-7 is a good number and add it to bath water. Do not take a bath in this, but soak for 15-20 minutes at least. Think only positive thoughts. You can say a prayer or just have happy thoughts. When done, air dry if possible, instead of using a towel.

After you finish, put one White Candle in your bedroom and the other in the living room.

If you are in a one-room home put both candles in the room. Light them and let them burn down to the socket.

The next day, start using the House Blessing Soap until it is gone.

BLACK DOLL OF PROTECTION

Take two white sheets of paper and one black sheet. Carbon paper is best for the black sheet.

Cut a small doll shape out of the back sheet. Place this between the two white sheets.

Place all three under your mattress.

As you sleep or lay on your bed, anything that is negative will go into the doll instead of you. You will now be safe and protected.

Leave this under your mattress for a month. Starting from the date you utilized the dolls' energy.

At the end of the month, take the doll out and burn it completely to ashes.

Throw the ashes to the wind.

Repeat the same process again to keep it going.

This is excellent when you feel someone may be wishing you harm, or out of jealousy wishing you ill, or any other form of negativity.

BELL AND CANDLE

For protection and for banishing, you need a bell and a white candle.

Make sure the bell has a sound that is pleasant to you.

Light the candle and let it burn to the bottom.

Ring the bell three times as you walk around the area, focusing on your intent.

HEX-BREAKING TOAD

Take some of the herb called Toadflax (also known as Flax Weed), and hold it in your hand.

Repeat three times:

> Fire and Mars,
>
> Mars and Fire,
>
> Break this hex,
>
> I so desire.

On the third repetition, add: So Be It!

Carry it with you either loose or in a white pouch.

UNCROSSING RITUAL

Use 7 white candles. On the candles carve:

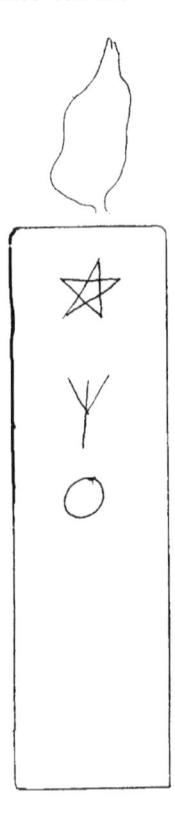

Do this starting on a Sunday.

Anoint with Jinx Removing Oil. Light the first candle only.

Sit in front of it and relax. Close your eyes. Visualize yourself happy. See negative energy going toward you, stopping a few feet away and dropping to the ground. You can think of it as arrows dropping on the ground.

Do this for at least five minutes. Then open your eyes and let the candle burn down to the bottom.

Do this for 7 days. One candle each day. Do not skip a day.

PROTECTION AT WORK

On white paper write this sigil in black:

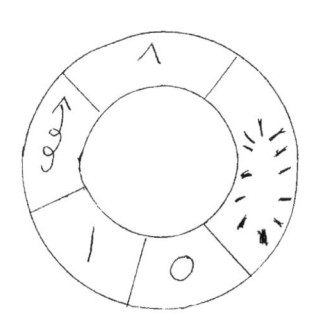

Write your name in the center. Concentrate on the purpose of the Sigil-as protection from <u>ALL</u> things for you.

Now write "Odin" in the center with your name

Call on his help to protect you.

Fold it two times and place it in your pocket or wallet. Carry it at all times.

If you have a desk, put a little pepper in it.

If you can, sprinkle a little pepper in the room you work in.

BANISH NEGATIVE PHONE CALLS

To banish or tone down negative phone calls, do the following:

On a small piece of yellow or white paper- you can also use Stick-On-Notes- draw an outline of a person. This person is you.

Draw a smile on the face.

Draw an oval shape around the body to surround it completely.

This is your protective shield.

Place this under the phone or stick it to the bottom of the phone.

It does not need to be visual.

When you pick up the phone, stay friendly.

If this is a negative or annoying call, stay friendly but firm and hang up as quickly as possible.

UNHEXING

Start on a Wednesday

Use a Black Skull Candle.

Two green candles.

One white candle.

Anoint all the candles with Uncrossing Oil.

Light some High John Incense and burn it each day for seven days.

In a red bag-carry a Lucky Hand.

After you light the incense and have the red bag ready, light all the candles.

Light them in this order: white, one green, Black Skull Candle, other green candle.

Let all the candles burn for five minutes and say a prayer you make up for protection and unhexing.

Put the candle flames out in reverse order. Do not blow them out with your breath.

Do this for six days. On the seventh day repeat the ritual and let the candles burn until they burn to the bottom.

UNHEXING BAG

In a purple bag add:

>   Dandelion
>
>   Rosemary
>
>   Clove
>
>   Basil
>
>   Mistletoe
>
>   Witch Grass
>
>   Devils Shoestring

Carry it with you at all times. Sleep with the bag near you.

SAFETY

To protect yourself against accidents, carry the herb known as Feverfew.

THE GUARDIAN

The Holly plant is utilized for protection in all forms.

It also guards you from lightning and poison..

Plant it near your home to protect it.

TOBACCO MAGICK

Before you travel by water, throw some tobacco into it to have a safe journey.

Tobacco Incense is used for protection and protection from spirits.

In magick, tobacco is used as a substitute for sulphur and nightshade.

Tobacco is considered very lucky and protective if you carry it.

Native Americans use tobacco for purification and protection at ceremonies.

PROTECT YOUR LUGGAGE

On a white paper, with red ink, draw a circle with the following sigil:

Put one in each travel bag to ensure its safety.

It increases the chance of it being safe, undamaged-with property inside the bag and of not getting lost.

As an example: it might have a little dent but it was not ripped open. There was a slight delay getting it, but it was not lost.

Usually it totally avoids a problem. It definitely improves what could have happened.

KEEPS NEGATIVITY OUT AND WEAKENS NEGATIVE PEOPLE.

Mix:

    Red pepper

    Cayenne (a stimulator)

    Sea salt

Sprinkle the mix around the house. Keeps negativity out.

Affirm:
"Any time I go in or out, it makes me and ones close to me clearer, stronger and more protected."

ANCIENT PROTECTION RITUAL

Take Squill (also known as Sea Onion) and hang it over your window.

Take some Sea Salt and add it to a glass of water. Dip your finger s into the water and trace the door and windows on the frames.

Sprinkle a little of this water on the threshold of any entrance-doorway-to your home.

PROTECTION OF MARS

Use Broom in spells dealing with protection or purification.

You can add it to a blend or ritual or use it on its own.

Hang it in your house for protection.

Make a tea of it and sprinkle it around your home.

PROTECTION OF WATER CRAFT- BOATS-SURF BOARDS, ETC.

Visualize a circle of White Light surrounding your craft.

Next, visualize Gold Light surrounding the white.

<u>Incante</u>;

> I now call forth the protection of Neptune, the Elemental Kings of Sea & Wind. Protect this craft and all who are in it from journey's start to journey's end. So be it.

In case of a problem, visualize the shield again.

SHIELDING

<u>Top View</u>

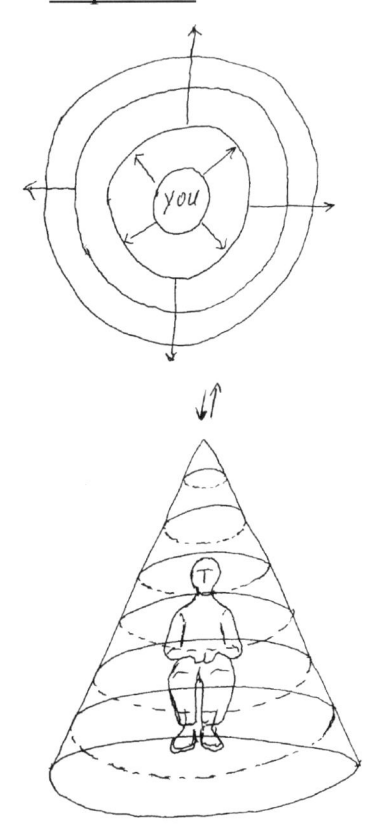

Sit comfortably in a chair. Relax. Visualize sending energy from within yourself outward in disk form.

At the same time, bring the energy down through the top of your head, your Crown Chakra, out through your feet and back up again.

You can picture the energy as White Light of protection.

TO SPOT AN ENEMY

Sprinkle some Sea Salt on your doorstep, on the threshold.

If anyone is an enemy, they will not come in, or be uncomfortable or edgy while they are inside.

It then becomes easy to spot.

HEIGHTEN ABILITY OF PSYCHIC LEVELS

Carry the herb called Broom and the Lapis Stone at all times.

You can place it in a purple or blue bag.

CHAPTER FIVE

FORMULAE FOR ATTRACTING LOVE AND ROMANCE

Love is the strongest Universal Force. It has unlimited power and should be utilized with care.

You can bring a new romance into your life, or an old one back. If the object of your affection stays or not depends on you both. The spells bring in the contact, not forcing it to work permanently once the contact is made.

There are various forms of love, affection and friendship. Make sure you stay on the positive side of all situations and intent.

RITUAL TO BRING LOVE IN

Use a Pink Square of material or pink handkerchief.

In the center put some soil.

Add:

1. The <u>name</u> of the person that you want to come into your life

   or

   If you do not have a specific person in mind, then put <u>my Right Partner.</u> Write this on white paper with black ink.

2. a rose quartz stone

3. a rhodocrosite stone

4. violet flowers

Tie it closed with five knots.

Light a pink 7-Day Candle and hold the pouch over it.

    Focus your intent.

    Invoke the aid of Venus:

> Oh, Venus of the Loving Flame,
>
> Your feminine energies are requested today.
>
> Fire and Water,
>
> Air and Earth,

Bring to me my mate on earth.

Bring (him/her) in a Positive Way,

Bless me with this, as I now say.

From dawn 'till dusk,

From dusk 'till dawn,

Work your magick,

One hundred strong.

So Mote It Be!

Let the candle burn to the socket, Throw away any wax that is left (outside your home).

Place the pouch under your bed and leave it there.

Start this on a Friday. Each Friday hold the pouch in your hands and repeat the invocation. Then place it back under the bed.

Do this until your desire comes in.

TIGER LUST

Utilized for the purpose of stamina in the male. Stimulator.

Fill ¾` of an 8 oz glass with Guinea Stout
Add 3 teaspoons sweet condensed milk
1 raw egg

Beat together. Drink it immediately. It is to be taken thirty to forty-five minutes before becoming intimate.

LOVE MAGNET

Blend these oils together:

>Gardenia

>Jasmine

>Clove (small amount)

Wear 2-3 drops every morning. Go out with a happy, positive, loving attitude. You are now pulling love into your life. You can use the oil before going to meet new people, in crowds, etc.

SENSUAL VIBRATIONS

Burn Rose Incense in the room, when you want a sensual mood. Your partner will react to the scent.

LUST OF THE GODS

Burn Vanilla Incense and wear 2-3 drops of Vanilla Oil on your throat and 3rd eye. Put 1 drop in your palm. Rub your Palms together.

MAGNETIC POWER-TO ATTRACT MEN

Blend the following oils and wear a drop or two daily (especially before going out):

>Ambergris

>Jasmine

>Lavender

Focus on your intent as you put this on pulse points.

MAGNETIC POWER-TO ATTRACT WOMEN

Blend the following oils. Wear the oil each day and before making contact with women. Put a drop on the palm of your hand. One on your throat and one on your heart. Combine:

>Musk
>
>Civet (a little)
>
>Bay (a little)

Focus on your intent when putting this on.

FIDELITY IN LOVE

Carry a Bohemian Topaz stone at all times. Give one to your loved one to carry in the same way.

ELIXIR OF LOVE

In a clear glass of water, place a red Ruby stone. Put the glass in direct sunlight for at least a day. Take the stone out and give your intended the water to drink.

It will heighten the level of feelings.

COLOR OF LOVE

When you want to attract love into your life, wear the color green or pink.

FRIENDSHIP

When you want to attract new friends or connect better with the ones you have, wear the color pink. Also wear something made of copper.

COMMERCIAL LOVE POTIONS

Many of the drinks that are now served at gatherings, nightclubs or at someone's home, were used as love/lust potions for centuries. Even though they were called love potions, what they really heighten are the sexual urges. Used consciously, this can be positive.

If you are already in a relationship, as an example, it will just be fun!

<u>Goldwasser</u>- a spice liqueur considered a curative, as well as virility Producing.

<u>May Wine</u>-sweet white wine. Contains woodruff

<u>Sloe Gin-</u>a liqueur from the sloe berry, also known as blackthorn. The sloe berry is found in many ancient ingredients for potions.

<u>Metaxa-</u> a liqueur that is brandy based.

<u>Vermouth-</u>a wine. Contains many of the herbs in ancient love positions.

EXCITEMENT OF LOVE

Invocation:

Hear me Deities of Love! Hear me Hera and Osiris!

Thou spirits of Venus! I desire to excite love and passion in the Heart of (<u>fill in the name of the person. If there is no specific person, say-my partner</u>).

Work your magick so my love is returned three fold

Work this for me if it is positive and good for all!

I conjure this command thus!

Az Istennel És Hathor! So Mote It Be!

The best day to do this is on a Friday or on a Sunday.

EROTIC ATTRACTION SPELL

Do this on a Friday.

On a pink candle, carve the following symbols:

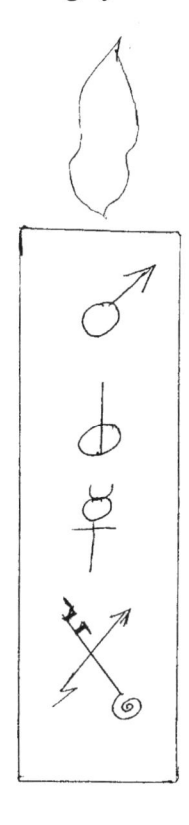

Sprinkle some Lover's Oil on the top and some Red Clover.

Sprinkle a little Love Powder on the top also'

Visualize what you desire clearly.

Light the candle.

Light Mush Incense.

Invoke:

> I invoke the candles forces through the God and Goddess. Bring about the outcome that I desire in a Positive Way. Let (name of person or if nobody specific, then say- the Right partner) come to me NOW. Let nothing stand in our way. Heighten the

erotic energies. Fulfill my desire. Thank you God and Goddess.

So Shall It Be.

Let the candle and incense burn down. Wear Musk Oil each day. Especially prior to going out.

This is a positive spell. To be used as an example: to intensify a physical part of an already ongoing relationship; if you do not have a partner but want one who is also sexual beside being a caring person.

RUNIC SIGIL FOR FIDELITY

On white paper, in red ink, draw this sigil:

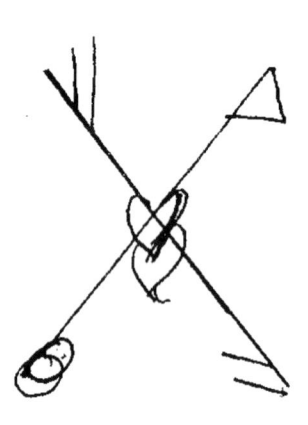

Focus on your intent while you write.

Underneath the Sigil, write both your names so that they blend. Example:

ANN and JOE

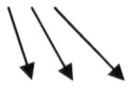

AJNONE

You can both carry one. Or put one under the mattress on his/her side of the bed.

COME TO ME

Start on a Friday.

Get a pink 7-Day Candle that pulls-out.

On the side of the candle, carve:

    the name of the person (or if unknown as yet-"my partner")

the following sigils-

(Six lines go above the magnet symbol)

Anoint it with Come To Me Oil-Rub the oil on the candle from the middle to the wick and the middle to the bottom.

Burn Rose Incense.

Light the candle and incense. Focus on your intent. Leave and let it burn to the bottom. Visualize the person coming to you on and off until it occures.

POPPET OF LOVE-NEW

Get pink material and cut out the shape of a person. Just a head, body, arms, legs.

Sew it closed, leaving an opening at the top to the head.

Fill this with:

    a Rhodocrosite stone
    a Moonstone

The herb-Patchouly

Orris Root

The herb-Red Clover

Sew it closed. Rub some Patchouly Oil on the doll. Focus your intent as you hold it in your hand and say:

I invoke the Goddess Venus!

Come to my aid!

Bring me my true love and mate!

Bring him/her now!

In a positive way!

So Mote It Be!

Place the poppet under your bed and repeat the invocation once a week on a Sunday.

ORRIS ROOT RITUAL

Take whole Orris Root to the closest body of water. Helps you to find your new love. Hold the root above the water and say:

Orris Root! Love drawing power! Bring my new love to me! I call on the aid of Isis, Aphrodite, Artemis and Ceres! Hear me! Make this a talisman of love and attraction!

As I will, it now shall be!

So Be It!

Walk away and carry it every day. You can place it in your pocket, wallet (if it is flat enough), or pocketbook. Also sprinkle some Orris Root on your bed sheets or between your mattress and boxspring.

The Orris Root powder is also called "Love Drawing Powder". If you can't find the powder in a store, simply use your mortar and pestle to grind some of the root to powder

INCREASE LOVE

In a cauldron, at the bottom, place the picture of your intended-facing up. If you do not have a cauldron, use any container you can light a fire in (a large ashtray or a bowl with aluminum foil covering the whole inside).

On the picture, sprinkle some of the following herbs/flowers:

Primrose, Rose petals, dried Elm leaves, Cinnamon and Vervain.

Light the herbs and the picture. As the flames consume them, focus and say 3 times:

As the sun turns in the day,

And the moon turns in the night,

(Name of the person)'s love for me,

Will never subside.

Visualize the love increasing. Visualize this until everything is ash. If the flame goes out, relight it until you are done

Take the ashes outside and sprinkle them to the wind.

It is done.

PASSION

Carve on a red candle the following sigils:

Anoint the candle with Musk Oil or Musk Perfume and focus your intent.

Let it burn to the bottom. Throw away any wax that is left to the winds.

EGYPTIAN LOVE TALISMAN

Empower this pouch/talisman with your will power and focus. As the petitioner, do the following steps:

1- <u>Talismanic pouch</u> -

   In a pink pouch add:

   Pinch of Vervain

   Vanilla Bean

   Rose Buds

   1 Rose Quartz-anointed with Love Oil

2- 6 red 4" candles

   Light one each day and let it burn to the bottom.

3- Write an affirmation for your needs.

   Example: Positive love to come to you Now.

Place the pouch in front of the first candle. Light it and read your affirmation three times.

When you have finished reading, leave the pouch in front of the candle until it burns out. Keep the paper for the lighting of the next candle.

When the candle is finished, take the pouch and carry it with you at all times. Any remaining wax should be buried in the ground.

Light one candle per day and read the affirmation. You only need to place the pouch with the candle on the first day.

On your last day, add:

Through Divine Power, So Mote It Be!

Carry the pouch until the completion of your petition.

WOMEN ONLY-LOVE/LUST SPELL

Rune binding is done in red. You can write it on white paper or on a small stone, or on a piece of wood that you will be able to carry.

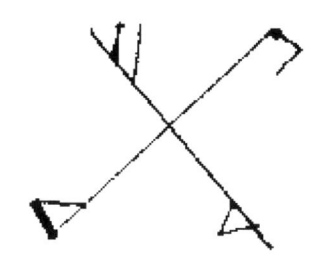

TREE OF FERTILITY

Find a yew tree. Ask it for its permission to utilize it. Wait a minute to see if you feel good or not about using it. If not positive, pick another yew tree and ask again.

Once you have your tree, use your knife to carve the following on it:

THOR, ULLR, FREYA

Place your palm on the area of the tree that has the writing

Petition the helping forces:

Thor, Ullr and Freya! I call on you to increase my fertility for the purpose of (say why you want this- children, sexual pleasure or whatever your peronal reaon happens to be). I call you forth until this work is completed!

Thank you Thor, Ullr, and Freya.

Thank you yew tree.

So Be It!

Walk away knowing it is done. Do not question the outcome or you will cancel it!

FAIRIES-BRING REALMS OF LOVE

Take a red apple and cut it in half. On one half carve the name of the person you desire and your name. Do the same on the other half.

Tie the pieces together with a pink cord. Use three knots.

Place this on your altar or on a table. Place your body in the following stance facing south:

Feet shoulder width apart, hands with fingers pointing skyward so your body looks like an "X". Put your head back, eyes closed.

Stay in this position for at least a minute or until you feel a sensation. Such as tingling.

While in this position, state what you want. Use the person's name on the apple, as well as yours. Add: Fairies of the earth unite, help me in this lover's plight.

Point both your hands/fingers toward the apple. Visualize White Light and your desire flowing from you, down through your arms, out through your fingertips and into the apple.

Take the apple and bury it near the base of a tree.

As it disintegrates, the energy is put out to the Universe and comes back to manifest.

BUTTERFLY SPELL-TO CHANGE A SITUATION

Get a picture of a colorful butterfly. You can usually find one in magazine, stickers, or you can photocopy one-in color-from a book.

On an unlined sheet of white paper or poster board, glue the picture. The brighter, the better.

Somewhere on your sheet, draw a pentagram in a circle. Write the persons' name that you want the change to happen with. Write what the change is.

Put a spiral drawing in black ink on the sheet.

The symbols are in the chapter of the book containing symbols and charts.

Focus visually on the butterfly for 30 seconds to a minute. Then read your purpose.

Repeat the visual part with the butterfly. Add the words:

Through Divine Power, In A Perfect Way, This change is now occurring!

Put the sheet somewhere where others will not see it.

Each morning and each night take it out and repeat the spell starting at focusing visually. Do this until the change happens.

Since ancient times, the butterfly has always represented change. One of my clients used this method to bring in a new love a few years ago. Not only did it work in record time, but he is now happily married with wonderful children. Not only is he happy, but because he did it in a positive way, his wife is also very happy with him.

HUNGARIAN LOVE MAGICK

To each cup containing red rose petals, add 2 ½ cup distilled water and ½ cup vodka.

Mix. Let steep for a week.

Strain. Add some more new petals.

Use this blend to splash on your body or to scent your bath.

It is utilized in love magick and to bring harmony.

PEACH SPELL FOR LOVE

Take a whole peach. Make sure it does not have any cuts in it.

Put three cloves in it on the outside, to form a triangle, pointing up.

Go to a large body of water and chant three times:

> Peach and water connect your forces,
>
> To bring a new love to my doorstep.
>
> Bring a love that's true of heart,
>
> So we'll have happiness from the start.

Then toss the peach into the water as far as you can throw.

SALAMANDER POWER

Build a fire outside, such as a campfire. As you wait for the flames to build, write your petition on a piece of paper.

Look into the flames and look for a salamander shape. At least one flame will have that shape if you look for it with sincerity.

Invoke its power, as you throw the paper in the fire:

> Salamander of fire and flame,
>
> Your power I wish to now attain.
>
> Bring the right love now to me,
>
> Activating force come to me!
>
> Come to me!

Let the fire burn out by itself.

LOVE SPELL

Anoint a red candle with Love Oil.

Say the incantation for five nights in a row.

Repeat three times:

I am possessed by love that is burning for (name) and I want (name) to have this same burning for me and me only. Let this come from Spirit and enter (name). Let (name) desires me as never before. (Name) must feel this same feeling as I feel. Spirit of the Air and Fire let (name) burn for me and not rest until we are together.

So Be It.

ATTRECT NEW FRIENDS

Wear Sweetpea and rub a little lemon on your wrists each day.
After they come in, it is up to you to keep it going naturally.

LUSTFUL LOVE OF THE AGES

Carry Ginseng Root on you at all times.

Make a strong tea of Ginseng to induce a powerful lust. You can make it by itself or blend it with other herbs for tea.

LUSTY MARS

On a piece of white material, draw the sign of mars in red ink in the middle:

♂

Take some Grains of Paradise and sprinkle some onto the cloth.
As you sprinkle it, <u>say</u>:

God of Mars and fire,
Come now to my aid.

> Bring love and lust into my life,
>
> As I now ordain.

Rub the Grains into the cloth a little. Fold it up and carry it with you.

Wear something visually red for the next five days. It can be something small, such as a handkerchief with the tip showing or jewelry with red.

THE ORCHID SPELL

The Orchid flower promotes love when worn or carried.

Place an Orchid root in a pink pouch.

Anoint it with Love Oil.

Hold in your hand and say:

> I call forth Venus; to grant my wish. I desire (fill-in what you want) to come to me now. Through the Power of Venus, I now thus command!
>
> So Mote It Be!

THE GENIE SPELL

Take an empty bottle to the ocean or a large body of water.

There find a small stick (male energy) and place it in the bottle.

Find a small seashell or round stone (female energy) and place that in also.

On a piece of wood or stone, write your desire. Add this to the bottle. "See" the outcome.

Next, go to the water and fill the jar. If you are at an ocean or where water flows to the shore and back out, fill the jar as the water flows toward you. Toward the shore. Keep adding water until the jar is full.

Hold it in your hands, look out toward the water and evoke the genie called Osoa:

> I now evoke Osoa!

To bring my desire of love to fruition.

I conjure thus: (fill in your desire. Make sure it is positive

for both people or it will backfire and cause you

problems. If you are not sure, add: I want this only if

it is positive for both concerned)!

Bring me this positive outcome Now

Stay with this work until it is completed. Thank you

Osoa!

So Be It Now!

Put the lid on the bottle. Throw it as far as you can into the sea/water. Throw it when the water is moving away from you.

Walk away and forget about it. You'll notice you have a happy feeling. Osoa will work on this for you however long it takes. A day, a year or whenever depending on what your desire was.

If you want a new love and do not have a specific person in mind, use the words-my Right Partner.

AIR AND EARTH MAGICK

First, find a feather. If you have tried and can not find one, the n buy one at a store. Many craft stores have them.

Go to a place that has sand or clear dirt (not covered in grass). You will need to be able to write in it.

Make sure you know exactly what your intent is.

Sit on the ground. Done on a Friday, it will heighten your effectiveness.

With the tip of the feather, write in the sand or dirt. Write your desire with focus and from the heart.

When done, add the words-So Be It!

Reread what you have written three times.

When you have finished, use the feather to obscure your writing. Wave it back and forth over the ground until you can no longer read it.

Take a little of this dirt home with you. You can place it in an envelope or anything that is convenient.

Place this under your bed.

FLOWER OF LOVE - To Make Love Grow

Acquire a Rose, Jasmine, Lily or Daffodil plant in a pot of dirt.

Write on a white paper with red ink:

> The love of (fill in name) now intensifies for
>
> me.(Name) can think of nothing else but me until
>
> (name) realizes how much I really love him/her. As
>
> this plant grows, so does our love, in a positive,
>
> healthy, happy way.
>
>   So Mote It Be.

Give the plant a little water and plant food. Take care of the plant. As the plant grows, so does your love.

EROTIC LOVE TALISMAN

On a piece of copper, draw with the color Back or engrave into it, the following:

Place the talisman on a flat surface or on your altar facing South.

Stand in an X position. With your arms and legs spread apart.

Say the evocation with purpose and feel the energy (or simply know it is there), flow into `your hands.

Evocation:

> I now call forth Orif! Fill this talisman with the energy of erotic love. Now! Activate its forces in this talisman. Magnetize this Talisman with the power of erotic love!
>
> Orif, I call on your powers.

Then wait a few seconds, aim your finger tips down toward the talisman. Feel or know the energy flowing from you, into your talisman.

Then <u>say</u>:

> Orif, do this now! Now, go forth.

Put your arms down and stand in your normal stance.

Carry or wear this talisman when you want its power.

Use it in a positive way. Such as heightening a love relationship you are in.

When not utilizing the talisman, wrap it in a cloth of white and put it away.

When done correctly, the talisman will be active for the next 80 to 90 years.

If for some reason you want to deactivate it, bury it deeply into the ground and leave it there.

POWER OF DRACOS

To attract love into your life, blend the following oils:

> Lotus, Juniper and Vervain (a little)

Put 1-3 drops on your throat and heart before going out. Focus on being loving and love coming to you.

IMAGE MAGICK

To attract love into your life, get a potato.

On the potato, carve face-that smile. Also carve the words-My new partner comes to me- (put your name).

Any thin sharp point is good to carve words, such as a thin knife or pointed pencil.

Hold it in your palm. Use your power hand-the one you write with.

Repeat:
>   Intense energy of the Moon,
>
>   Bring my new love now to me.
>
>   Perfect, positive mate to be,
>
>   Let the love flow
>
>   So mote it be.

Wrap the potato up in brown paper and place it under your bed.
When it gets dried out, bury it in the ground.
The best time to do this is at night, from the New Moon to the Full Moon. At the Full Moon, bury the image.

SPELLS OF LOVE

The herb called Myrtle can be added to any love pouch, love spell or to increase love that is already there.

Wear it while performing love magick to heighten its magickal power.

FAIRY FIRE SPELL

Perform this ritual at dawn.

Light a small fire. It can be a campfire, a few papers in a large ashtray or cauldron or any form convenient to you as long as it is outdoors.

Look into the flames as you sit by the fire. Stare at the flames until your vision becomes unfocused.

Ask the fairies to appear to you. You will either 'see" them or just know that as you call, they do appear.

Talk to them, the same way you would to a friend and tell them what you desire. Ask them for their help in obtaining what you want.

Thank them for their help.

Let the fire burn out on its own.

Take a little of the ashes and carry them with you. You can place them in a pouch (red), envelope or loosely in your wallet.

Scatter the rest of the ashes.

HAPPINESS IN LOVE

Utilize the herb known as Witch Grass.

To attract new love and to be happy, sprinkle some under your bed. Each week, replace it with new Witch Grass.

You can also carry it at all times.

CIRCLE OF LOVE

Either draw a circle clockwise in the ground while standing in the center or form a circle with others. You need 13 or less people.

<u>Solitary</u> - Focus on what you desire, knowing that as in a circle, you are surrounded by love and simply need to focus on what you want. Wherever you are, the circle always "comes around" and brings what you want. It will do so, but in its own time. Fast or slow, the results come in. Trust it.

After you focus, <u>say</u>:

> My desire is (<u>fill in your need</u>) and it comes to me
>
> now. Trough the power of the Goddess in her Triple
>
> Form. Through the Divinity in all of us, in a way that

is Perfect. Goddess, hear my desire and activate your Force. Thank you Goddess. Go forth until this work is done.

>So Mote It Be!

Reverse the circle, then leave.

<u>Group</u> - Stand in a circle, holding hands. Stand for a minute in silence, focusing your desire.

Have a <u>leader</u> say:

> Our desires are focused and now we say.

<u>Group</u>- in unison repeat what is written for the solitary worker. When you get to the part where you fill in your desire, pause silently for a minute to give everyone a chance to say their desire silently. At the end of the minute or two, the <u>leader</u> needs to start verbally to continue so others can join in.

When completed, let go of the other persons' hand and leave the circle.

GINGER OF POWER

When performing love spells, eat some ginger. The vibrational energy will heighten the love spell.

DRAGON SPELL OF LOVE

Dry some Lime peel. In a cauldron or fire-proof container, add to the Lime peel some Cinnamon, dried Chamomile, dried Rose (any part of the plant) and some Love Incense.

Light these and say with your intent clear:

> Dragons' fire,
>
> Dragons' flames,
>
> Burn all opposition in my way.
>
> Bring the Light of loves' true flame,
>
> To manifest what I want in my name.
>
> So Mote It Be.

When all is in ashes, throw the ashes to the wind to bring about the manifestation.

ALTAR OF ROSES

Set up your altar to heighten love, bring new love or intensify lust.

Be clear before you start on what your intent is.

Altar:

```
┌──────────────────────────────────────────────────────┐
│  ○ Pink          ○ White              Red ○          │
│    Rose            Candle             Rose           │
│                                                      │
│                  ○ Rose                              │
│                    Incense                           │
│    Red                                Pink           │
│    Candle                             Candle         │
│  ○                                         ○         │
└──────────────────────────────────────────────────────┘
```

You can place the roses in any clear vase with water. Otherwise, add a few drops (3) of water on each flower.

If you use an altar cloth, do so in any one of the colors represented by candles.

Light the incense and say:

> I consecrate this space that I am working on as Sacred
>
> Space. Protected and Powerful.

Light the red candle, then the white, then pink.

Say:

I light the flames of (fill in –love, new love,etc). My desire is (fill in purpose) and it manifests 100 fold. My clear path to my desires is now lit with brightness and happiness. The Light of my Inner Flame is also activated to do, in a positive way, what is needed to accomplish my desire. I ask for the knowledge to do the Right things to bring this in. I ask, knowing the answer is already given.

Let everything burn out by itself and walk away.

Any time you have an urge to do or not do something, a hunch or an intuitive feeling, move on it! Trust it! Do it! You asked for the information, now you have to follow through when it comes to you.

SPELLCRAFT OF THE MAGI

Take an apricot and squeeze the juice out.

Dry the apricot and on the inside of the skin, write your petition of love.

Then dip your index finger into the juice and trace the edge of the skin with the juice. As you anoint the skin, focus on your intent.

When you are finished, dig a hole and pour any remaining juice into the bottom. Next, add the skin. Cover it with dirt and walk away.

-If you can not write on the skin, write your petition on paper and wrap it in the skin. Tie a white thread or cord around it to keep it closed-

TREE SPIRITS - ATTRACTING YOUR MATE

At the roots of an Elm tree, sit quietly for a few minutes and get an awareness of the area. Do you feel at peace? Are there happy people near such as in a park? Are people upset? Does the tree look healthy?

If you get a positive feel, use this tree. If not, get up and find another one.

Then do the same.

Once you have the tree, on a piece of white paper with green ink, write the qualities you want in a mate. Take your time. Include everything important to you. After all, nobody else will see your personal list.

When you are done, wrap the paper (you can fold it up) in an elm leaf.

Dig a little spot for this near the roots. Bury it.

Then ask the help of the Elm and the Spirits of the tree to come to your aid. Tell them exactly what you want to manifest in your love life.

Thank them for their help and walk away.

LEMON WISH FOR FRIENDSHIP

Take a whole lemon and make sure there aren't any cuts or dents on it.

Tie a pink ribbon on it, after wrapping it around the lemon four times.

Focus on new friendships coming into your life.

Wrap this in pink cloth. Tie it with pink thread.

Hold your palm over the lemon and say:

> New friendships now come unto me,
>
> Come by air or land or sea,
>
> I am open to the new,
>
> Friendships come if you are true.
>
> As friends come in,
>
> A friend I'll be,
>
> My heart is open,
>
> For all to see.
>
> As I will,
>
> So Mote It Be!

Take the lemon and throw it into the water as far as you can. Any water will do.

Make sure you are friendly, open and smiling to other. It is safe to be open.

STOP INFIDELITY

To put a stop to this situation, put a piece of Turquoise, Moonstone, Rose Petal and High John The Conqueror Root under his/her pillow when you go to bed together. You can place them separately under the pillow or in a pink pouch.

As he/she sleeps, say"

> Through Divine Power, Aphrodite and Isis, you will be true to me always. Your love will grow and we work out all problems easily and happily. In a Perfect Way.
>
> So mote it be.

CANDLE OF DESIRE

Each night at sunset, light a red candle.

As you light it, say:

> Red candle, red candle,
> Of my desires.
> Burn with these flames,
> Higher and higher.
>
> And as the flames,
> Shall flicker and die,
> My desires to this Universe,
> Are sent by design.

Then focus for a minute on your specific desire.

Say thank you to the fire energy and let it burn down to the bottom.

Do this until your desire is fulfilled.

LOVE AND HARMONY

Do this to bring love, happiness and peace to your home.

After any time when an argument occurs, burn Rose Incense in the room(s). Where you burn this incense, calm will prevail. It will prevent the negative energies from staying in the room. It will not be able to build so that it sets off arguments.

Have you even noticed how some rooms make you feel uncomfortable without a logical reason?

That is because vibrations build up and you feel the negativity. You can feel it in a number of forms. Such as anxiety, being edgy, uncomfortable or restless.

This will take away any outside interference.

Next, wear something visually pink. Men can use a handkerchief sticking out of a pocket. It does not have to be large.

Wear this color for a while and work on improving all situations to bring balance and harmony.

Wear rose perfume or for men, wear musk.

INSPIRE LOVE

Put some of the Lovage herb into a pouch made from muslin or other open weave material. Put this in your bathtub under hot running water. When the water is 1/3 full, add enough cold water so you can bath in it comfortably.

Soak in the water and think happy thoughts.

When you are in a go mood, get dressed and go out.

This will make you more love inspiring to others. You will attract them.

BRING NEW LOVERS

On a piece of paper write your wishes.

Wrap the Paper around a chestnut and carry it at all times.

SPIRIT OF LUSTFUL PASSION

In a red bag put some of the following:

    Vervain-herb

    Rhodocrosite-stone

    Pink Agate-stone

    Job's Tears-herb

    Red Clover-herb

On the outside of the bag, in red, write:

♂ ⚡ ☿ ♀ ☸

Focus on your intent when you write.

Carry the bag at all times, especially when going out.

MANDRAKE-YOUR HEART'S DESIRE TO COME BACK

For bringing back a past love.

Take a Mandrake Root and carve his/her name on it.

On a piece of parchment, write what you desire as an outcome.

On the paper draw:

☸ ✦ ✛ - <u>Name of person</u> ◯

Wrap this around part of the root. Tie it with a red ribbon.

Focus on your intent.

Put it in a safe place where others will not touch it.

Take it out each Sunday, talk to it and tell it what you want. It is not a request, it is a statement-I want....

Do this until the person comes back.

This is not to make him/her stay-once back. That you have to work out naturally.

MOUNTAIN MAGICK

At dusk, stand in a place where you can see the top of a mountain to create love magick.

Look down and collect a few small items from the area. Such as a pebble, leaf, twigs feather or nut.

Hold these in your hands and look at the mountaintop

Say:

> As I look up at this mountain as it reaches to the sky, so must I reach for my desires. I desire (fill in what you want). I want this in a positive way. I know it is already coming to me.
>
> I give these offerings to represent my sincerity. To also do all I can to have the desires I strive for happen.

Now throw everything to the South Wind. (Face South)

Thank the Forces of the Mountain for the help.

Walk away.

PAN-EARTHLY LOVE

Add a little water to the earth to be able to shape a figure. If this not workable, use some clay-gray or brown or any earth tone. For any love desire.

Form a doll from the clay.

On it, draw a mouth (smile), nose and eyes (open).

On the heart, draw a heart big enough to write your initials in. Then add the initials.

On the throat and groin area, draw a circle.

Across the chest write his/her name (or my new partner).

On the Third Eye – or the center of the forehead-write PAN.

Hold the doll or place it on your altar. Focus on what you want. Add that- PAN helps you in your magickal work to effect the heart of (name) for the intent of (fill in).

When you are done, <u>say</u> - Thank you Pan.

Take the doll and bury it.

As it goes back to the earth, so your desire manifests

LANTERN OF LOVE

To bring in a new love.

You need to find an Elm or Willow or Oak tree.

Get a lantern or flashlight.

A thin piece of paper (so the light can shine through)/

Cut the paper so it will fit over the glass part of the lantern.

On the paper, draw:

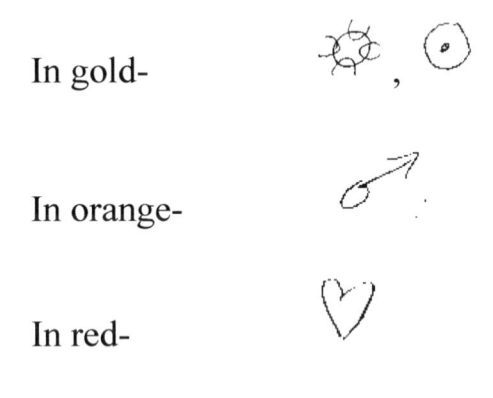

In gold-

In orange-

In red-

In black- all else

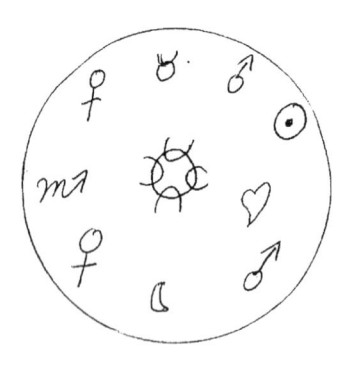

On the night of a New Moon, place the picture over the glass on the lantern (you can tape it.) Go to the tree and shine the light on it so the sigil is visible on the tree.

As you see the sigil, focus on your desire and how it will be when you have what you want. How happy you will feel. How loving you will be. Where you will both go or what you will do together. Be focused on it a if it already happened.

Allow yourself to relax and look at the sigil on the tree.

Shut the light off.

Disconnect the paper and burn it to ashes'

Bury it near the tree. Thank the tree for working with you to bring about your desire.

Walk away.

Go back one week later and pour a little water on the tree at its base. Day or night.

LOVE ATTRACTION TALISMAN

To attract love and heighten positive emotions toward you, make this talisman.

On a disk shaped piece of wood, draw:

Carry it with you at all times.

The best time to make the talisman, is when the moon or sun is in Taurus. You can make it at any time if this is not workable when needed.

WHEN LOVE MUST COME TO YOU

On parchment or white paper, use Dove's Blood ink. Write the name of the person you have in mind seven times (do not use capital letters, or cross letters or do I's-Example: Kristin is Krıslın).

Make a mixture of anything sweet and add some spice. Such as: honey, cinnamon stick, brown sugar, white sugar, cloves.

Get a small bottle or jar. Put in the first layer of the mixture, then the paper and something that belongs to the person who you want to come to you. (Hair, beard, or thread from clothing would do). Put the picture facing up. Then put second layer of the mixture on top.

Blow your breath into the bottle, call his/her name and say what you want him/her to do.

Put the cap on tight. Love must come to you.

You must keep the bottle warm. It is best wear it on your body. If you can not, then hold it between your hands in (or under) warm water about 15-20-minutes a day.

Works within 7 days.

TO GET SOMEONE TO SHOW LOVE

Anoint a pink Seven Day Candle with Love Oil. Rub the oil from the middle to the wicks' tip, then from the middle to the bottom.

Sprinkle some brown sugar on top.

Write the name of the person you want on a piece of paper and place it under the candle.

Light the candle and let it burn to the bottom.

TO COOL OFF TEMPERS

Put some ammonia (very little amount) in an open jar under the person's bed.

MAGICK MIRROR

To get someone to come to you, get a picture of him or her.

Tape it on a mirror or behind it.

Tell him/her what you want him/her to do. Example: call, come over…Talk to him/her. This person will come to you.

FOR SOMEONE TO COME TO YOU IN A POSOTIVE WAY

Repeat on and off with conviction:

"I demand to have (name) come to me in my favor".

RABBITS' FOOT FOR LOVE

Get a red rabbits' foot.

Place it on a red cloth.

Sprinkle it with Rosemary.

Put three drops of Love Oil on it.

Close the cloth by folding it.

On each Friday, focus on what you want as you hold the rabbits' foot.

Sprinkle a little more Rosemary on it.

Fold it in the cloth again.

When you are done, place the cloth in your dresser or with your clothing until the following week.

Repeat this each Friday.

EYE CONTACT SPELL- TO BRING SOMEONE IN

This can only bring someone in if it is meant to be.

Look directly into his/her eyes, while repeating silently-" You are mine and I am yours, while visualizing how delicious you will be within each others embrace.

This takes one or two direct contacts if it is right and on time.

CHAPTER SIX

DRAWING THE CORNUCOPIA OF LUCK INTO YOUR LIFE

Luck is a combination of many things. Of timing, the vibrational effect on you or other things, your outlook on life, to name a few things.

Have you ever noticed how some people will say they are always lucky? And they are. They expect it, they know it as a certainty, they feel it.

If they do have a loss, they do not worry. They know this happens once in a while, but they know they will be lucky soon, as expected.

So keep a positive attitude. Know you will be successful.

The Law of Supply is on your side.

See which type of method works for you the best.

If you have an instinctive urge to do something differently-DO IT. Your psychic/intuitive ability and information always outweighs everything else.

If you have a method that works for you-keep it. You can add new ones on.

There isn't any conflict in utilizing more then one method. As they are all meant to bring various forms of luck to you, they work in harmony with each other.

Have you ever thought anyone had too much luck? Of course not.

Luck, prosperity, health, love, happiness are all our Divine right.

God wants us to be happy. Look at parents as an example: your mother (Goddess) and father (God) always want what is best for you. They want you to do well. To be happy in life. How could they want anything less for us?

Sometimes we may want something not good for us, or not good at this particular time-like candy before dinner or going out at a time when you are too ill.

In that case, we may not get exactly what we want. However, we will wither get something else that is the same or better or we will get it at the right time.

It all works out as luck and success.

Stay happy, focused on the positive and help others when you can.

Remember, luck is at your fingertips!

LUCKY RABBITS' FOOT KIT

You will need one orange rabbits' foot,

>Luck Oil

>Small magnet or drawing one

>An herb-Grains of Paradise

>A green cloth

Anoint the rabbits' foot by running a few drops of Luck Oil on it.

In the middle of the cloth, put everything else.

Add a few drops of the oil on them. Close the cloth and tie with green string or ribbon. Use five knots to close it.

Carry the pouch and rabbits' foot at all time to increase your luck.

Anoint the rabbits' foot once a month at a New Moon.

LUCKY MONEY MAGNET

On a piece of paper draw:

At the center of the magnet-where the smile is, put a picture of your face. You can glue or tape it on.

See the luck coming to the magnet (you).

Fold it up and carry it in your wallet or purse.

SHOWERS OF GOLD

As you stand under the water in your shower, close your eyes.

Picture the water a gold and success. Picture it in a form that is fun and that you are comfortable with.

See it as the water being gold. Or gold coins. It can be golden opportunities of success.

Do this every morning and every time you need this success before going out.

Go out with confidence, feeling happy and lucky.

IRISH LUCK

Find a four-leaf clover. Carry it with you.

WINNING HORSE RACES

Before you go to bet at any races, do the following:

Make an elixir by putting the gem stone called Lapis Lazuli (washed off) in a clear glass. Add water and put it in direct sunlight in the morning.

At night prior to going to sleep, take the stone out and drink the water. You can do this up to an hour before going to sleep.

Before you sleep, say:

> I want information that is clear and understandable to me, that I will remember until I write it down, on what horse will win at (fill in with day, race, etc).

Then get some sleep with a paper and pen next to your bed.

You will have very vivid, clear dreams.

When you wake up, write down your dreams immediately.

When you look at the sheet with the names of the horses running (in the information you asked for and wrote down) a name will have a connection to your dream. That is your horse. As an example: if you dream about castles and the feuds then look at a newspaper or racing form and find a horse called White Knight-there is a connection!

GOOD FORTUNE

Wear the Turquoise stone at all times to bring good fortune and increase luck.

ORANGES OF LUCK

To attract luck and good fortune, take a whole orange and place it in your home. Wear the scent of the orange to attract the vibrations to you of luck and fortune. If you are in a warm climate, plant an orange tree on your property.

LUCKY LIFE

In a white bag combine:

- Alfalfa
- Chamomile
- John The Conqueror Root
- Cloves
- Mandrake
- Vervain
- Lode stone
- Mistletoe
- Jasper-gemstone
- High John Powder

Put five drops of High John Oil or Luck Oil on the bag.
Close the bag with five knots.

LUCKY PLANET

On a piece of tin, draw or engrave your name and the following signs:

[symbols]

Draw seven short lines in the horseshoe.

Carry it with you.

GEM OF POWER

Hold a Carnelian stone in your hand and say:

>Lucky gem from beneath the earth,
>
>Come magnetize my life,
>
>Luck with money,
>
>Luck in life,
>
>Lucky gem you are now mine.
>
>>So Mote It Be!

Carry it or wear it.

ALL-PURPOSE LUCK

In a white bag blend:

- Holy Herb
- Khus Khus
- Chamomile
- Vervain
- Orris Root
- Alfalfa
- Jasper-stone

Tie it closed with seven knots. Focus on your luck increasing as you do this.

Hold the bag between your palms and focus again.

Carry it or wear it around your neck.

LUCKY BATH

Make a tea from Cinnamon.

Put the tea and a clear Quartz Crystal in your bathtub. Fill it with water.

Soak in it for 15-20 minutes, at least. Do not wash or use soap.

When you are done, let your body air dry.

Take the stone and carry it for luck.

LUCKY NUMBERS

Pick some numbers. The ones in your birth date are very good, in any combination.

Write these in orange on white paper.

Write your name.

Take this to a tree and bury it near the base.

Ask the tree to help manifest your desire. Say what that is-To be lucky with these numbers (fill in).

LUCK AND GAMBLING

On a green candle on a Sunday, carve:

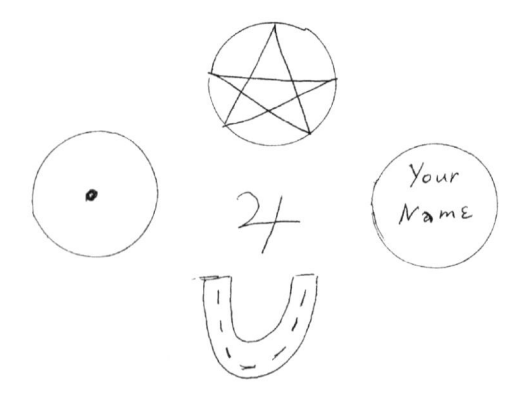

Light the candle. Let it burn to the bottom.

Take a small piece of the wax that's left to carry and bury the rest.

LUCKY STONE

On a flat stone of Jasper, Turquoise or Apache Tear, draw the following symbols in black or red:

(Seven lines in the horseshoe)

Use a clear wax or clear nail polish over it so it does not come off.

When this is dry, carry it.

Touch it before playing games of chance.

ELEPHANT ENERGY

Buy a small elephant statue. Make sure the trunk is pointing upward toward the sky.

Place the elephant so that the tail faces your front door.

It will bring luck to your house.

WORD OF POWER

When you need money coming to you fast, especially if it is through games of chance, repeat the word-TRINKA several times.

LUCK ATTRACTION

On an orange candle, carve:

Light some Allspice for incense.

Light the candle and let it burn to the bottom

Thank the tree and walk away.

BALL OF LUCK

Burn down an orange candle until it is soft. Or put it into a warm spot until it is soft enough to mold.

When it is moldable yet cool enough to touch, add to a flat piece of it the following:

    Jasper- a small stone

    Fenugreek

    Cloves

    Orris Root

    Holly Herb

    Chamomile

    Alfalfa

Sprinkle a little Shower Of Gold Oil or Luck Oil on it.

Form it into a ball, with everything in it. Place the gemstone showing near the surface. Keep it in your room.

LUCKY BOWL

Place a little cotton in a sugar bowl to attract luck.

HOLLY

Carry some Holly to bring good luck.

Due to the plant being considered a male plant, it is especially lucky for men.

Hang it in your home for luck.

When planting Holly near your home (it also protects), repeat the spell three times during the planting.

Say:

> Holly bush of Mars and Fire,
>
> Bring protection and Luck as I desire.

After the third repetition, add - So Mote It Be.

FREYA-GODDESS OF LUCK

Carry the leaves of the Strawberry Plant to attract good luck.

Before you start carrying the leaf, say the following while holding it in your hand:

> I invoke the aid of Freya,
>
> Luck for me will now abound,
>
> Sacred leaf of Goddess Freya,
>
> Magnetize luck all around.
>
> So Be It!

THE FAIRY WOODS

Go into the woods for this Luck Ritual.

Make a fire and in front of it, in the dirt, draw:

As the fire burns, say:

    Fairies, Fairies, come to me,

    Change my luck for all to see.

    All luck now changes to good,

    The fairies help I now invoke!

When you are done, thank the fairies for their help.

Take a small leaf or twig and leaf and brush away the picture.

Let the fire burn at least another minute. Then you can put it out.

ALTAR OF LUCK

On a flat surface or altar, place a white cloth.

On top of it place an orange cloth, that you will later carry.

Follow the altar placement:

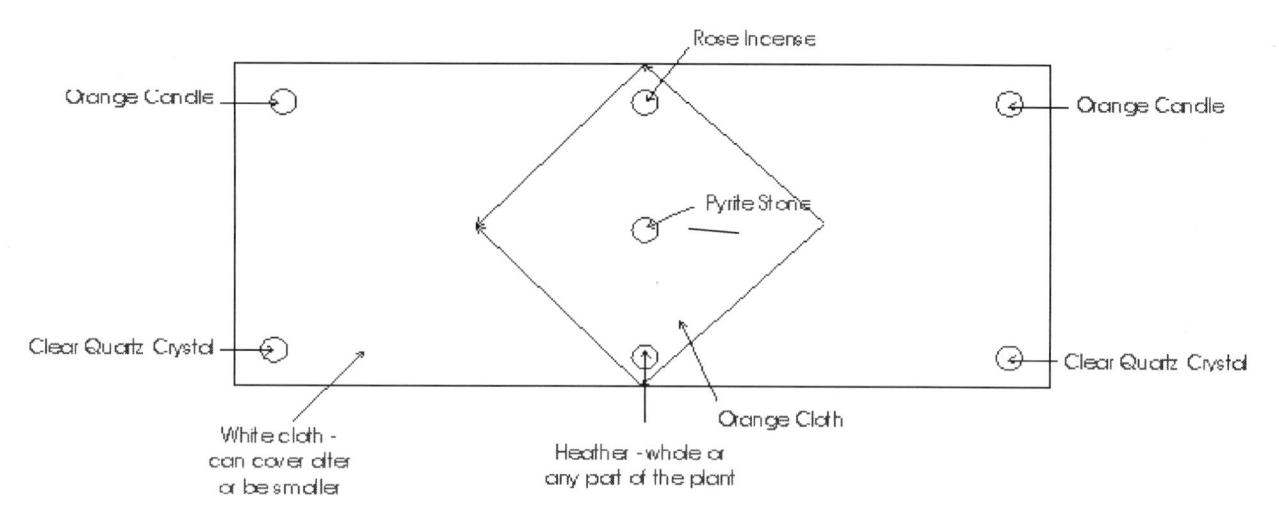

Altar diagram showing: Rose Incense (top center), Orange Candle (top left and top right), Pyrite Stone (center), Clear Quartz Crystal (bottom left and bottom right), Orange Cloth (diamond in middle), Heather - whole or any part of the plant (bottom center), White cloth - can cover altar or be smaller (underneath).

Light the Rose Incense then the orange candles.

Focus your intent on attracting luck in all forms to you. See yourself as a magnet. Feel the energy from the altar flowing into you.

Stand with your body in an "X" position. Arms and legs spread part.

Say:

> I now invoke the Goddess Isis! Bring luck to me now, Energize my altar for this purpose. Magnetize the Pyrite and Heather to bring unlimited luck to its owner.
>
> Through the Power of Isis, through the Force of the Divine, I now have the luck that is from the Gods.
>
> Thank you Isis. So Be It!

Let the candles and incense burn out. When they are all out, take the Pyrite and part of the plant and wrap it in the orange cloth.

The plant or pieces can be placed in your bedroom.

The cloth should be carried with you.

HELP OF THE GNOMES

Go outdoors where there is a mountain, yard, hill, park, forest or woods. If you are unable to do this, buy an Aloe Plant that has an abundance of dirt in the pot.

Stand outdoors or in front of the plant.

<u>Repeat</u>:

>I now invoke the Elemental King!
>
>I know you by name.
>
>Come to me <u>Ghom!</u>
>
>Bring luck to my endeavors.
>
>You, oh Great King,
>
>Who inhabit the earth's interior,
>
>I call upon you.
>
>Come to my aid so that luck will now be mine.
>
>Let it flow from the earth
>
>Let my energies synchronized with luck.
>
>>Thank you King Ghom and Blessed Be.

When you are finished, walk away.

LUCKY BATH

In a bathtub filled with water, add some dried pineapple pieces, along with some of the pineapple juice.

Soak in the water at least for 15-20 minutes.

Do not take a bath with soap, just soak.

Visualize your luck increasing. As the waters' vibration soaks into your skin, so does luck!

SPIRIT OF THE EARTH

Go to a place where you can draw in the sand or earth.

Draw:

▽

Put your hand on the symbol, palm down.

Visualize the symbol of the earth glowing with green light. See or know the light becoming more and more intense.

See an outline of orange around the symbol.

See the symbol and colors rise up and go into your hand. Leaving a glowing mark. Focus on luck coming to you.

Stand up and rub out the symbol on the earth. The symbol will stay in your hand.

When you need extra luck, especially with money, feel, see or know the symbol is glowing on your hand.

Allow it to glow, then forget about it and let it dim again.

THE POWER OF BLACK

Black represents power and force. It gives the ability to banish negative energy and spirits. It is not necessarily negative, as most people assume. You choose how you want to use it.

When burning candles, I find burning a white candle at the same time, ensures it working on a positive level. Of course, it depends on what spell you are working. It may not be needed.

On a white piece of paper (to keep it positive) with black ink (to add force and power), write the following:

▽ ◎ 🛡 ☘   Your Name-
                " I NOW HAVE CONSTANT LUCK"

Fold it two times.

Put it in a cauldron or a container that you can burn things in.

Light the paper and <u>say:</u>

>As the ashes rise higher,
>
>This ritual fulfills all my desires.
>
>Luck now comes into my life,
>
>From dawn to dusk,
>
>From dusk to dawn.
>
>I am LUCKY from now on.

Make sure all the paper is burn to ashes. Relight it if you need to.

Take the ashes outside of your home and throw it to the wind.

A few times each day, <u>repeat</u>:

I AM ALWAYS LUCKY.

Once you have done this ritual (and repeated the words for a while), you will actually see a difference in your life.

I had a client a few years ago who did this ritual. Financially he was doing all right, but not too well. Nothing was really improving. Mainly staying the same, day in and day out. He wanted to improve his life, but could not decide what area he should tackle first and how.

Within a few months of this ritual (he was still repeating the words), he had an urge to play the lottery. He followed the urge and won $ 300.00. He was happy

And felt his luck was changing. Again on a hunch, he went to a class to try something new and met a woman he immediately liked, asked her out and now had a date. A few months later, he got a raise on his job. Much earlier then he expected.

A little at a time, his life was turning around. He was much happier. He also became accustomed to expecting good fortune in his life, instead of thinking it only happens to others.

Sometimes luck comes in very fast or dramatically. You never know how it comes in, only that it does.

LUCKY OILS

Date Of Birth	Oil
December 22-January 19	Gardenia
January 20-February 18	Carnation
February 19-March 20	Violet
March 21-April 20	Sweetpea
April 21-May 20	Lily of the Valley
May 21-June 21	Rose
June 22-July 22	Honeysuckle
July 23-August 23	Cherry Blossom
August 24-September 23	Wisteria
September 24-October 23	Musk
October 24-November 22	Jasmine
November 23-December 21	Magnolia

WISHING CANDLE

Get a green 7 Knob candle

Each day, starting on a Sunday, burn one knob.

Light the candle and focus on what you want. When the first knob burns down, put the flame out. Do not blow on it to do this.

The second day, repeat the ritual.

Do one each day until they are all finished.

LUCKY TALISMAN

Get a green or orange stone that has a hole going through it.

Hold it in your Power Hand (the one you write with) and say:

> Stone of Power,
>
> Three times Three,
>
> Luck shall always come to thee.

Repeat this three times. The third time, add the words:

> And as I will,
> So shall it be!

Carry the talisman with you at all times. It will attract luck to you. If you are more then three feet away from it, then it will work for whoever is closest to it.

The best time to do this work is at the New Moon.

A CHARM TO DRAW LUCK IN GAMBLING

On your altar or a flat surface, place the following:

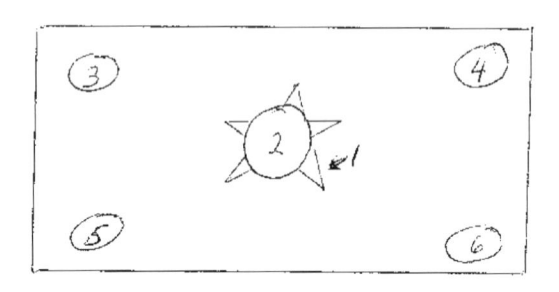

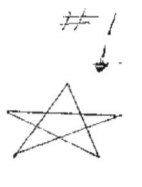

1- Draw a pentagram on white paper and place it in the center.

2- Place Rose Incense on top of the pentagram.

3- Place a white candle. Anoint with Luck Oil.

4- Place a white candle. Anoint with Lucky Oil.

5- Place a green candle. Anoint with Lucky Oil.

6- Place a turquoise stone or a lucky charm that you have in this position. Anoint it with a drop of Lucky Oil.

Get some gold sparkles (craft and party stores also carry them). Sprinkle a few on the top of the candles.

Light the incense first.

Light the candles in order: 3,4 then 5.

Affirm:

I am the God and the Goddess. I am always lucky. This charm brings good fortune to me. I am Luck incarnate!

Let the candles and the incense burn out on their own.

When they are finished, take the charm and carry it with you at all times.

On and off each day, repeat the affirmation as you touch the stone.

You can leave it in your pocket, touch it and say the affirmation silently, as an example:

DOUBLE POWER

In a red pouch, put 2 (a pair) of Lodestones, carry it or place near your bed, to drive evil away and attract good luck.

TALISMANIC ENERGY

Draw or carve the following in wood or tin.

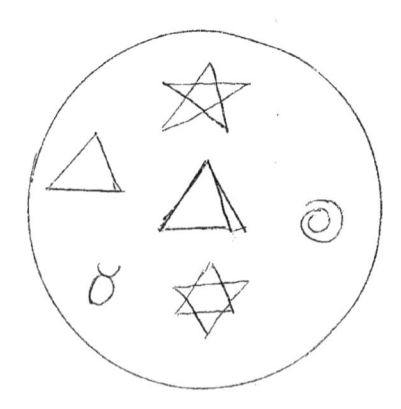

On the back, put the Sigil of Jupiter. Found in the chapter of symbols.

Anoint the talisman with Luck Oil or Rose Oil.

Sit alone for 15 minutes with the Talisman in front of you or in your hand

Relax. Clear your thoughts. Relax and breathe in three times slowly.

Think of luck being yours. Feel lucky. Visualize situations where you are happy because something lucky just happened for you. Make it personal. Example: You got a raise on your job, `bought something for yourself and took your family or friends out to dinner.

After you did this for at least the 15-20 minutes, take a deep breath. Then slowly open your eyes.

YOUR OWN PERSONAL BAG

Make your own Luck Bag that is meant only for you.

Get an orange bag (or cloth you can tie together).

In the pouch add:

- a small picture of yourself
- a little hair
- a Jasper stone
- a Nutmeg
- a piece of tin

Close the bag tightly with 8 knots.

Hold it in your hand and think of White Light going from your hand into the pouch as you say:

> This personal bag now brings me luck. I automatically make the Right choices to gain luck in all areas of my life.

Carry the bag and repeat what you said every day. At least once, the morning being the best time.

LUCKY NUMBER BAG – FOR GAMES OF CHANCE

First you need a white bag.

Write numbers on separate pieces of paper. Such as from 1 to 100.

To this bag add:

> Grains of Paradise
>
> Turquoise-small stone

Anoint the bag with High John Oil.

To use:

Put a little of the High John Oil on your hands. Rub them together.

Shake the bag.

Open the bag. Free your mind from daily thoughts. Relax. Concentrate on what you need the numbers for. Example: I need my lucky numbers for the lottery (say how many numbers you need and any other relevant information), for the Stock Car Races (in detail) or any other form.

Reach in the bag.

Pick the numbers. One at a time. Lay them down in front of you in order.

Write the numbers down. Then place them in the bag again.

Put the bag in a safe place.

Carry it to bet or gamble.

GAMBLING HAND

Take a whole Nutmeg of India and drill a hole in it. Do not drill all the way through on the bottom.

Into this hole, pour some liquid mercury.

Melt wax over it to seal it.

In a red bag, place the nutmeg when the wax is completely dry.

Add:

>Magnetic Lodestone (2)
>
>High John The Conqueror Root
>
>Five Finger Grass

Sew the bag closed with red or white thread.

Put one drop of Success Oil on the bag.

Put the oil on the bag one time each week.

BINGO BAG

In a green bag add:

>Turquoise stone
>
>Job's Tears-herb
>
>Cloves
>
>Nutmeg
>
>Small horseshoe

A picture of a Triskelion

A picture of a Four Leaf Clover

Grains of Paradise

Put some High John Oil on each. Concentrate on winning as you do each. Picture yourself happy and with a smile.

Keep your focus as you close the bag. Tie it closed with 8 knots.

Carry the bag with you.

Rub your hands with a few drops of the oil as you go to play Bingo.

When you have your Bingo cards, put a dot of the oil on each of the four corners. Start at the top left corner and go clockwise.

STONE POWER

Carry Botswana to attract money in games

FOUR LEAF CLOVER AND EGYPTIAN SCARAB FOR LUCK

The four leaf clover is a very old symbol of luck, while the Scarab is utilized to attract finances. Together, they are a powerful force.

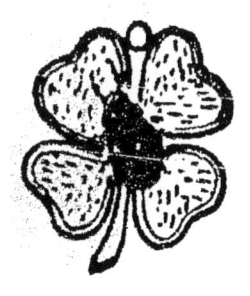

Make a copy of the talisman. As you look at it, say your petition:

I now call on the force of the Sun, Earth and Hathar. I (fill in your name), call on you to activate this talisman, to bring luck my way. Bless this talisman for the purpose of (fill in your petition or say-for bringing luck to me).

Thank you for your blessings and power.

If you would like to, you can attach it first to cardboard or wood. Something to make it sturdy. Or simply fold it and keep it in your wallet.

BRING LUCK

Take a white rabbit's foot and rub the soles of your shoes with it to bring luck and success wherever you walk

LUCKY NUMBER CANDLE

Buy a green candle. Sprinkle Fenugreek on top.

In a green bag, put seven Job's Tears,

Use High John Incense.

On a piece of paper, write-what you want or desire, seven times.

First put the paper under the candle.

Place the bag in front of it.

Light the incense, then the candle.

Focus on your desires.

Let the candle and incense burn out by themselves.

Then pick up the bag to carry when you need it, or at all times.

FAST LUCK

Get a horseshoe or horseshoe in miniature form.

Anoint it with Lucky Oil.

Anoint a green candle with the same oil.

Focus on the outcome when you anoint both.

Use Luck Incense.

Hold the horseshoe as you light the incense and candle. Place the horseshoe next to the candle.

Let the candle burn for one hour, then put it out. Do not blow on it.

Let the incense burn out by itself.

Put the horseshoe in a safe place.

In three days, repeat everything. Concentrate on your desire.

In another three days repeat the ritual.

Concentrate. This time, let the candle burn out.

The horseshoe is now your good luck charm.

It is now activated.

I find that a Seven-Day Candle works very well for this ritual, but you can use any size.

LUCKY GAMBLERS WASH

This ritual has been utilized by gamblers for centuries.
Make a tea from Chamomile. When it cools down, wash your hands with it before you gamble.

GOOD LUCK IN ALL THINGS

Keep a Peony plant in your bedroom or the room you spend the most time in.

Take a little piece of the plant, let it dry out and carry it in your wallet or pocketbook.

HOME OF THE ELVES

Sprinkle some Alfalfa in your kitchen cabinets to attract luck to your home.

Sprinkle some in each corner of your rooms.

In each room as you do this, <u>invoke</u>:

> Good Elves of the deepest forests, I invoke you!
>
> Bring luck to this house and all who dwell within.
>
> You will always be welcome here. Thank you!. My
>
> home is now overflowing with luck.

Visualize your house glowing in WHITE from so much luck.

FLOOR WASH

Make your house lucky. Add some Van Van Oil to a bucket of clean water.

Wash your floors with it to bring good luck. Let it air dry.

PHOENIX SPELL

Utilize this ritual to change your luck to good.

Take a Seven Day Candle in green.

Also a Breakaway Candle of black and green.

Anoint both with Prosperity Oil. Rub the oil on the top clockwise from the outside to the tip of the wick.

Write or carve on the candle: <u>your initials</u>.

On a piece of white paper, write:

> As the Phoenix rises from the ashes,
>
> So does my luck change for the best.
>
> Everywhere, I attract luck, opportunities and abundance.
>
> I rise as the Phoenix to now claim my Rights!
>
> So Be It.

Put the paper under your black/green candle.

Light the candles and focus once again on the words with serious intent.

Let them burn down to the bottom. Do not put them out.

Walk away knowing your life is about to change to the better.

Make sure you keep a feeling of expectancy.

BINGO

Light a white candle.

Clear your mind of al daily thoughts and worries.

Visualize in detail-winning. If you can not visualize, think of all the details. Remember, there is power in the word! Verbal or non-verbal. As you visualize, keep focused.

Then shout-**BINGO!**

Think how you feel and how you will feel when you win.

You MUST truly believe and it will happen to you.

Success depends on belief, in knowing.

Look at the lit candle and say:

> My luck in BINGO is Rightfully mine.
> I desire and know luck is with me to win.

Burn the candle for one hour. Put it out. Do not blow on it.

Go play! Have fun.

FAST LUCK DOLL

Cut out a doll shape from pink material.

Sew around the edges, keeping a space open at the top of the head to be able to fill it.

Put the following into the doll:

- Pink agate
- Rose quartz
- Fast Luck Powder
- Khus Khus
- Chamomile
- Buckeye
- Peony

Sew it closed.

Light a pink candle and place the doll in front of it. Invoke:

> Spirits of the earth and sea send your Power and Luck into this doll for me.
> Spirits of the air and fire, Fast Luck is now my true desire.
> I now invoke your spirit forces to magnetize this doll for the purpose of fast luck.
> Thank you. So Mote It Be!

Let the candles burn out.

Take the doll, wrap it in pink cloth and put it away in a safe place.

Once a week, take it out and sprinkle some Fast Luck Oil on it.

NECKLACE OF PAN

To bring luck.

Use a purple cord, ribbon or other material you can string talisman on.

Find: a green leaf or a picture of it. Fold it.

Carnelian stones with holes going through them. (You can find them at Lapidary shops, hobby or craft stores, among other places).

Light a green candle while you string the stones.

It is very important to string either 3,7,8 or 9. Utilize these exact numbers.

When you are finished, cut the cord so that you can tie the ends at a comfortable length.

Tie it with 3,7,8 or 9 knots.

Put the necklace on when you desire luck or wear it at all times.

Take the leaf and place it in your wallet or purse. Leave it there at all times.

FAIRY STONE

Carry a piece of Amethyst for luck.

Hold the stone and look into it for a short time.

Your vision will unfocus.

As you gaze at the stone, ask the fairy who resides inside to show itself to you..

Sometimes you will see the fairy.

This stone brings luck.

GOOD LUCK CHARM

In a red bag carry some Star Anise.

Watch as your good luck charm increases your luck.

YOUR LUCKY SPELL

Place the following herbs-Cinnamon, Thyme and Chamomile with Rose Oil into your bowl.

Use Good Luck Incense and an orange or green candle.

Invoke the name of Huna and light the incense and candle while saying:

> As I now encircle myself in my White Light Shield, I call upon Huna to help me manifest (fill in your desire) in my life NOW.

Keep your focus on your desire for a little longer.

Let the candle and incense burn down to the bottom.

You can make a mojo bag with the mixture from the bowl. Use the same color cloth as the candle. Throw any left over mixture to the wind.

If you do not utilize the blend in a bag, leave it in your room in any open container.

WALNUT SPIRITS

Go to a tree that has walnuts growing. Ask the spirits of the tree if you can pick some leaves to attract luck in gambling.

Close your eyes, 1take a slow deep breath and wait a minute. If you do not have any uncomfortable feelings, then the tree spirits agrees.

If you do feel uncomfortable, thank the spirits anyway and move to another tree.

If this tree is fine, pick a few leaves and thank the spirits.

Go home and soak the leaves in Gambler's Oil for a few hours.

Take them out to dry until they are all dried out.

Put them in a pink pouch or leave them loose and sprinkle or put some in your wallet.

RITUAL FOR GAMBLING

Take a High John The Conqueror Root and place it on an altar on a Sunday.

Light High John Incense.

Light a Double Action candle for money.

Let everything burn down to the bottom on its own.

Take the root and rub it between your palms before gambling.

FLOWER OF LUCK

Take some Indian Posy and sprinkle some of it around each room of your home for luck.

MAGICK BEANS

Carry Mojo Beans (or 3 Nutmegs) with you to attract luck.

To add more energy to them, anoint them with Lady Luck Oil.

They may be carry in a purple pouch or cloth.

LUCK IN BUSINESS

Carry Wonder of the World (or Grains of Paradise) to attract lucky conditions into your life.

Carry it especially to business meetings, when asking for something such as raise or when looking for a job.

NEW JOB

On a Sunday, to get a new job, burn some Wood Betony with some Fast Luck Incense.

Focus on your intent. Such as, getting a specific job (always add-"or better') or if you do not know what you want, say:

> My Perfect, Right Job comes to me NOW, easily,
>
> effortlessly and quickly.

Then go out and look at the newspaper and do whatever you need to do on the physical plane.

At the same time, follow all your hunches.

You need to work on both realities to manifest your desires.

ALL-PURPOSE LUCK

Take some Bear Weed (also called Yerba Santa) and rub it on your shoes.

Wherever you walk luck opens a path for you.

WINNING STREAK

To win at anything, carry some Blue Gum (also called Eucalyptus).

Focus on your intent to win. See it happen.

Winning covers numerous areas, such as: love, business, gambling or a race.

BURNING BUSH

Carry part of the bush to attract luck.

Anoint it with Lucky Hand Oil and place in a red bag for added strength.

LUCK AT ANY RACE

Utilize this formula for any form of race. For example; horses, boats, cars or track.

On a large green candle, carve:

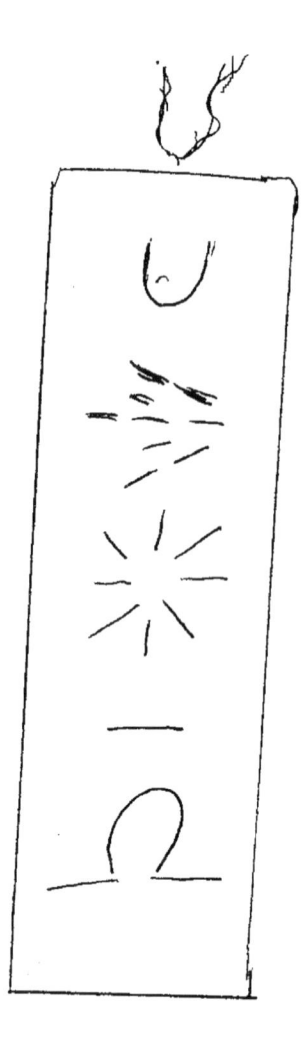

Sprinkle a little Alfalfa or Aloe on top.

Light it and concentrate on your petition. Be focused on winning at races for a few minutes. Then let the candle burn to the bottom.

You can now walk away.

When the candle is burned down and there is a little wax left, take some and carry it with you when betting or going to a race.

INCREASE YOUR LUCK

Draw a triangle large enough to place a bowl on. You can draw this on white paper. In the bowl put:

> Thyme
>
> Grains of Paradise
>
> Rose

Place the bowl on the triangle. (Pointing up).

On this blend, sprinkle some Rose Oil.

Burn some Rose Incense.

Invoke the Goddess:

> Triple Goddess come to me,
>
> By air or earth,
>
> By smoke or sea,
>
> Increase my luck 100 Fold,
>
> Your Force and Power I now invoke!
>
> > So Be It.

When the incense has burned out, take the mixture in the bowl and put it in a purple pouch or cloth to carry.

CANDLE MAGIC-LUCK IN LOVE

Do this on a Sunday.

On a pink candle, carve:

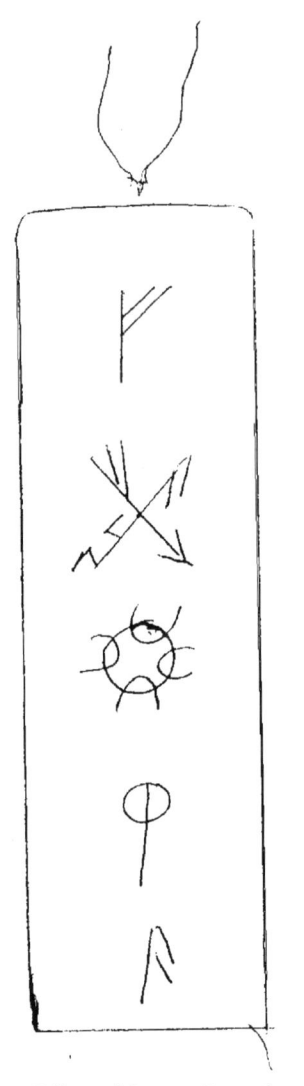

Anoint the candle with Love Oil and Love Powder.

Light the candle.

Light Rose Incense.

Focus on what you desire.

Invoke:

Freya, Goddess of Love and Luck, Bring my desire to fruition. Do this now and in a Perfect Way. My desire of love is (say your desire). Thank you.

So Shall It Be.

Let the candle and incense burn out by themselves.

When they are burned down, your manifesting has begun.

LUCKY NUMBERS-WITH SPIRIT'S HELP

Before you play the numbers or gamble with the use of numbers, call for extra help.

Hold a small statue of an elephant or a picture of one (trunk pointing up).

Invoke: after circling yourself with White Light!

I now invoke the help of the Triple Goddess to aid in my luck increasing-With the numbers.

I invoke the Spirit of the Master of the Lucky Numbers.

I want you to increase my luck and in a Positive Way.

I want to (say your desire-with specific types of how you want to use the numbers-such as lottery or Bingo).

Stay with me until this is done. Then go forth.

Put the lucky energy into this elephant.

Thank you Goddess, thank you Spirit.

So Be It.

Carry the elephant when you need its help.

FAST LUCKY NUMBERS

Burn Money Drawing Incense.

Light a purple candle.

Light an orange candle.

Sprinkle some Orris Root around your home.

Say:

> Powerful Spirit of Luck, send to me the good luck I need and want. Send it to me fast for lucky numbers. Send it NOW. Thank you spirit. Go forth when this is done.
>
> So Be It.

Let the candles and incense burn out on their own.

BLACK CAT OF LUCK

Carry a black Cat Eye stone or wear one for good luck.

LUCK IN A NEW VENTURE

Focus on your intent as you do the following:

On paper or a piece of wood, draw the following Sigil:

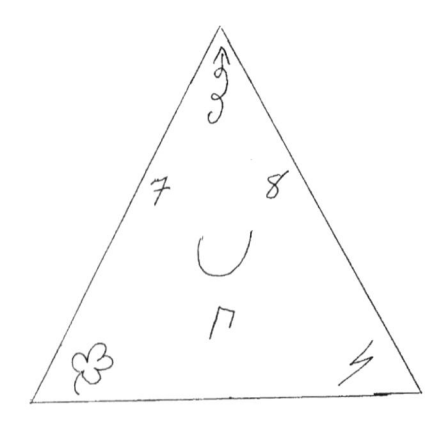

Sprinkle some John The Conqueror Powder on it or powder some Orris Root with your mortar and pestle.

Take your Sigil to the nearest water and throw it in as the water flows away from the shore. Focus on your intent as you do this.

LUCK IN TRAVEL

When you travel, take this talisman with you.

It will keep you safe. Even if there is a problem, you will be fine.

Keep it on your body. In your pocket, wallet, anywhere as long as it is physically worn.

Draw it on wood, tin or paper.

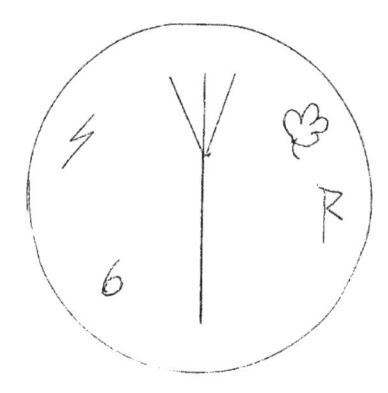

When you are not traveling, keep it in a safe place.

A client was traveling out of the country and took this talisman.

She felt safe knowing that it makes her safe, sometimes in unusual ways.

The flight was delayed by a few hours after everyone was seated on the plane. People were getting annoyed and restless. However, she was calm, knowing there must be a positive reason since she wore the talisman.

Later she found out that there were mechanical problems that they found just in time and were able to fix without a problem.

However, once in the air over the ocean, it would have been a different story since it would not have been fixable.

(Even in that case if the plane went down, she still would have been safe at the end.)

LUCK DRAWING

Pull luck to you by doing the following:

In a white bag, add:

> Agate-stone
>
> Turquoise-stone
>
> Seal-drawn in this formula
>
> Irish Moss
>
> Fenugreek
>
> 2 Lodestones

Anoint the bag with Lodestone Oil.

Close it with seven knots.

Anoint it once a week on Sundays while focusing on your desire.

The Seal

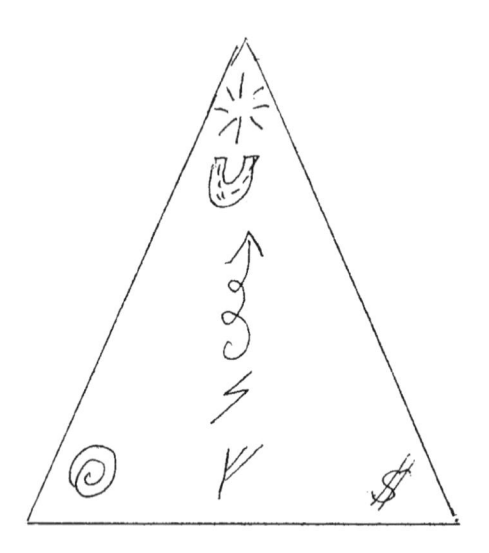

(Seven lines in the horseshoe.)

CHARM

Get a small black cat statue or a picture of a black cat.

Also a miniature horseshoe or picture of one.

Anoint both with a few drops of High John the Conqueror Oil.

Place both in a white cloth or pouch.

Carry this for protection and good luck.

BINGO BAG OF LUCK

In a purple bag, add:

    Jasper –stone

    Carnelian-stone

    Lucky Hand-herb

    Seal-drawn in this formula

    Grain of Paradise-herb

    Fern-herb/plant

    Star Anise-herb

Close the bag with seven knots.

Anoint with Money Drawing Oil and Money Drawing Powder.

Carry for luck.

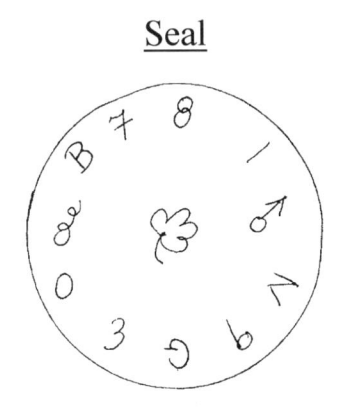

<u>Seal</u>

DRAGON'S LUCK

In a box painted orange, place these stones:

    Clear Quartz Crystal

    Turquoise

    Botswana

    Jasper

    Jade

    Apache Tear

    Amethyst

    Adventurine

Light Dragon's Blood Incense or Luck Incense.

Place the open box in front of it.

Light an orange candle.

Invoke:

    Dragon of fire, smoke and flame,

    These treasures I consecrate in your name.

    By fire you guard your treasures stones,

    Luck upon them is now bestowed.

    Shiny treasures to acquire luck,

    We share their power of luck, luck, luck!

Add:

    Thank you ancient dragon, now you can sleep.

Let the incense and candle burn out. If you use Dragon Incense, do so near a window or some ventilation. It can be strong.

Close the lid of the box. Put it somewhere safe.

When you need luck, open the lid. Do not look, but put your hand in and pull out a stone.

That is the stone, which will help you that day. At the end of the day, place it back

ADDED POWER

Add to any sachet, incense, candle or any ritual to intensify it's power:

Steel dust also known as Magnetic Sand.

PERSONAL LUCK

Put some Luck Powder on the palms of your hands and rub together.

Put a little on the soles of your feet.

On your Third Eye-found in the center of your forehead.

You can sprinkle some anywhere else on your body after these specific areas are done.

Focus on your intent as you do so.

Go about your normal day.

MAGNETIC LUCK WITH MONEY

On a purple candle, carve the following:

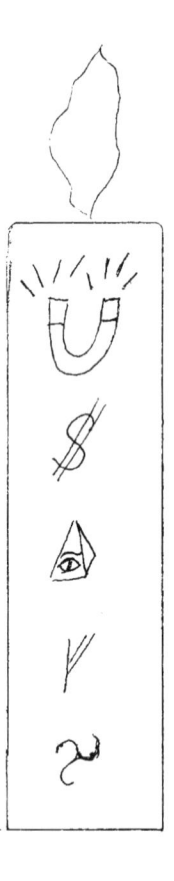

Sprinkle some Lodestone Oil on the top. Place 2 Lodestones at the candles base about one inch away. Place the stones next to each other.

Light the candle and focus on what you want.

Let it burn to the bottom.

Take what remains of the wax and bury it in the ground.

Take the two stones and place them in a purple pouch to carry or to place in your cash register or desk at work.

INCREASE BUSINESS

For luck and money:

Use this formula to increase your business if you own a store or your own place of business.

On a piece of wood, draw or carve this talismanic Sigil:

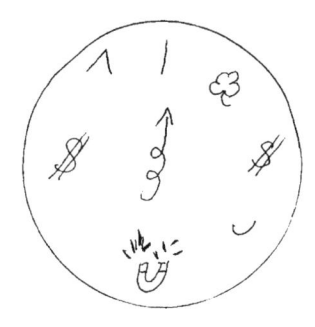

Take a piece of Orris Root and place it in the center.

Use green cord or ribbon and wrap it around both, to keep the root in place.

Tie it with nine knots.

Place it in your cash register (it can be placed in a green bag or cloth), or wherever you receive money.

Sprinkle some Alfalfa in the corners of your place and on your doorstep where people enter. On the inside so it is still <u>in</u> your place, not outside. This way people have to step over it to come in.

CHARM FOR LUCK IN COURT

On a piece of white paper, with black ink, draw this Sigil:

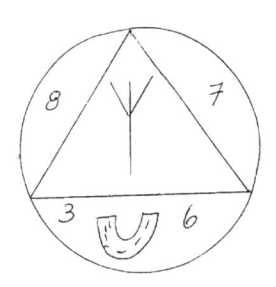

Write your name on the back. Focus on you being happy walking out of court. Know your outcome is successful.

It increases success in your favor.

Fold it in half and place it in your pocket or somewhere in your body.

Wear a pink shirt or blouse to court. It can be a very light, pastel color so with a man wearing it, it will still look serious.

If you can not get a shirt/ blouse, then wear anything that is pink where people will see it. Such as a scarf or a handkerchief sticking out of a pocket.

It will change the situation. As an example: if someone was normally given a 20 year sentence for what he/she did, now it would be 2 or none.

LUCKY CANDLE OF LOVE, SEX AND ROMANCE

On an orange candle, carve:

Anoint the candle on a Friday with Love Oil.

Next, light the candle.

Burn Vanilla Incense.

<u>Say:</u>

> Through Odin's might
>
> Through Aphrodite,
>
> My desires are met tonight.
>
> I want (<u>fill in desire</u>). In a positive way.
>
> So Be It.

Let the candle burn down to the socket.

Go out and wear a few drops of Vanilla Oil.

Wear something green.

And be friendly!

LUCKY DUCK

Place an image (toy or statue or any form) of a duck with its tail facing your front doors to attract luck to you and your home.

STAR LUCK

Carry Star Anise to bring luck. Place it in your home. Add it to luck spells to give added power.

ROOT TALISMAN

Carry the Snakeroot as a good luck attraction and to cancel someone wishing you negativity.

FAIRY DOLL LUCK

Take some straw and tie it together to form the shape of a doll.

Call for the help of the fairies to bring luck to you.

Place it in your bedroom or the room you spend the most time in.

Sprinkle some straw around your place of work, in your desk or in your wallet.

CHAPTER SEVEN

CREATING POSITIVE CASH FLOW TO ENHANCE YOUR PROSPERITY

Prosperity includes many areas of your life, money being one of them

Many times, when you think of someone who is prosperous, you immediately associate it with money and wealth. That is fine, since we are meant to have a happy life and that is part of it.

However, it also means being prosperous and growing as a family. A farmer is prosperous when the crops are good. We are all prosperous with health, love, food and safety.

Prosperity includes your whole life. You can not be prosperous if you have a negative attitude about yourself or your life. If you think you will never have money, you will <u>not</u> have it. You really do get what you ask for.

The universal energies that help you to manifest listen to what you say, not what you mean.

When you find yourself thinking thoughts of lack and poverty, quickly use the word "cancel" and immediately think of the same situation in a positive, abundant way. You want to replace the negative thought with a positive one.

Prosperity is not limited to cash. If you own a home, land, stocks, vehicles, material things, it is the same as cash.

When you are working on your intent, if you want money, affirm that you want-a specific amount or better. If you want a car, focus on the car, not the cash. In this way, you can get the car in any number of ways. Such as: they dropped the price so it is now more affordable and you can buy it; someone bought one for themselves and gave you the older car-which is still in a great condition; you received it as a gift.

We will be more focused on money in this chapter, but keep an open mind and work with other aspects on your own.

Prosperity is all around us, be open to it. You deserve it!

CAULDRON OF MONEY

In a cauldron or bowl, place the following:

On white paper, write with focused intent:

> Through My Divine Right, I now claim this money! I claim (fill in the amount) and more! For the purpose of (fill in purpose-such as a new car).
>
> I now call in the God and Goddess to activate this cauldron for money growth. Anything I put in the cauldron grows tenfold and more.

Then on the same paper write a symbol that represents your religion. If you do not have a sign, put a pentagram.

Put this at the bottom of the cauldron.

Sprinkle some Alfalfa on it.

Add a Pyrite stone.

Focus your intent and with purpose, say what you have written.

Put some folding money in the cauldron.

Every chance you can, including with small change, add to it for that specific purpose.

Anything you put in is only to be used for the one purpose.

When it looks full, take some out and change it to larger bills (five singles to one five dollar bill). Then put them back.

Keep adding to the flow. If you can not fit anymore in, take an envelope, write the "purpose" on it and put the money in it. Put the envelope somewhere safe.

Keep the cauldron going.

When you have achieved your goal, leave the stone in the cauldron with the herb (you may add more of the herb). Take the paper out. Rewrite it with a new goal. Repeat the formula.

AFFIRM

Take three slow breaths and relax. Focus on what you desire.

Affirm:

I always make the Right decisions to manifest riches into my life.

I always make the Right choices to attain, keep and build wealth.

I always choose the Right Path.

Say the affirmation each morning upon arising.

Put a copy of it in your wallet and mentally reaffirm at least part of it (time allowing) —or more, every time you see it.

Place it in your wallet so that you can at least see part of it as a subconscious reminder.

TALISMAN FOR BUSINESS AND SUCCESS

Make a copy of the Seal of the Sun. Contained in this book.

Anoint the corners with Successful Oil.

Carry it on your person. Said to do the following:

Helps heighten your ability to make decisions.

Aids in finding a job.

Character strengthening.

Success in all ventures.

When asking for loans or dealing with banks.

Owning a building (home or business).

Gaining a higher position.

PROSPEROUS HOME

Burn some Thyme in your home to bring wealth to everyone who dwells there.

Sprinkle some around your home.

BRING MORE MONEY TO YOUR BUSINESS

Take a Buckeye and wrap a one-dollar bill around it. Do this so that you can see the face on the bill.

Place this in your cash register or where you receive money.

Sprinkle some Myrtle around the rooms.

MONEY GROWING RITUAL

Sprinkle some Coltsfoot on your money and say:

> Vishnu I now invoke your aid!
> Help me to grow my money so that I may improve
> my life.
> Thank you.
> So Be It.

TREASURE HUNTING

Carry Black Snake Root to lead you to money, opportunities with money and treasure.

INCREASE BUSINESS, MONEY OR TO GET A RAISE

Focus on your intent.

Get a green candle and anoint it with Money Drawing Oil.

At midnight, light the candle and burn some Absinthe.

Let them burn out on their own.

MONEY ATTRACTION

Make a tea from Chia Seed and sprinkle it around the room.

MONEY TREE SPELL

Get a small plastic tree or some twigs to form a tree or make one.

On the tree, attach pictures of money. As you place each picture on the tree, say:

> Money tree, money tree,
>
> Grow for me,
>
> Money comes to me now,
>
> Easily and effortlessly.
>
> And as I will,
>
> So shall it be.

Place it somewhere where you will see it daily. It could be non-visual to others, such as at the bottom of your clothing closet.

Your money will now increase.

CANDLE OF DIANA

Carve on a white candle:

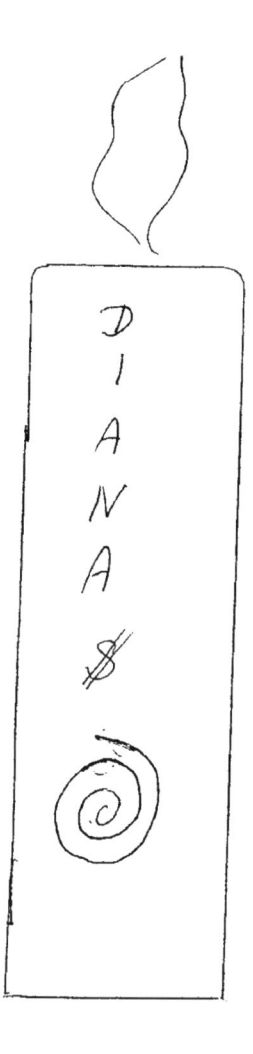

Anoint the candle for money and prosperity with Patchouly Oil.

Light the candle.

Burn some Money Drawing Incense with some Cleavers Herb.

Let them burn out on their own.

Take it to a lake, stream, ocean or any body of water and throw any remains from the blend or candle in.

Thank Diana for her help.

Walk away.

SEASHORE SPELL FOR PROSPERITY

Go to a seashore and find a seashell that you can draw on. Draw the following Sigils:

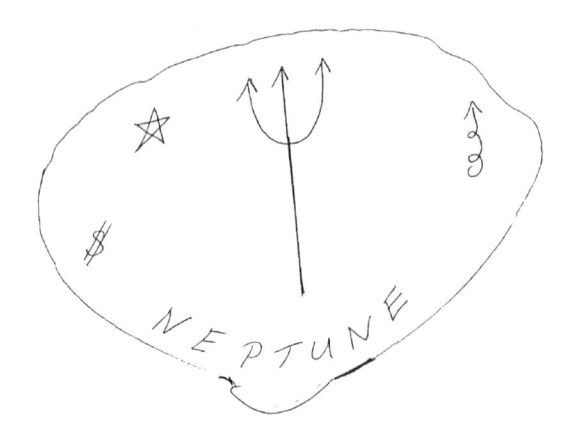

Go to the edge of the water and invoke the help of Neptune, God of the Sea.

Ask for his help in increasing your wealth and prosperity. Thank him.

Throw the shell back into the sea and walk away.

PROSPERITY MAGNET

Wear or carry the stone called Black Agate to gain prosperity.

RABBIT'S FOOT FOR MONEY

Get a green rabbit's foot.

Rub a few drops of Money Drawing Oil on it.

Sprinkle some Alfalfa on it.

Then rub your money with it.

When you are not using it, wrap it in green material and put it away in your dresser or closet. Near your clothing.

PROSPERITY DOLL

Cut a doll shape from gold colored material. Sew it closed, leaving an opening at the top to add magickal ingredients. Concentrate on your purpose.

Add:

Some nuts (3)

Oak leaf

Basil

Dill

Fenugreek

Sesame

Sew it closed.

Anoint it with Success Oil as you hold it in your hand.

Ask for the help of Kwan Yin for the purpose of (fill in).

Thank her for her help.

Place the doll in a safe place.

Take it out each Sunday and tell it what you want.

Put it back until the following week.

Do this until you reach your goal.

MONEY NECKLACE

To attract money, buy or make a necklace with a coin on it. Gold tone.

Rub the edge of the coin with Money Drawing Oil, going clockwise, each morning. Starting on a Sunday at sunrise.

Wear it daily.

ALL PURPOSE PROSPERITY RITUAL

Light a purple and a white candle.

Light Frankincense for incense.

In a small box, put some of the dirt near your home, pebble, leaf or whatever is near you.

Add 8 pennies.

On parchment paper, write and concentrate:

> I now accept my prosperity. I am a child of the God and Goddess and I now claim my Right to a prosperous life. I make the Right decisions to bring this about and I take Right action. In a positive way, I am the son/daughter of the God and Goddess!

Add this to your box.

When the candles and incense burn out, check to see if anything is left of them. Anything remaining gets added to the box.

Take white cord or ribbon, tie the box closed with 8 knots.

At the next New Moon, take the box and bury it.

TREASURE MAP FOR MONEY IN BUSINESS

On a poster board or white paper, put colorful pictures and slogans for what you have as an intent.

Put pictures of business men who have already made money'

Of men who have achieved a goal-that you admire. Such as: Tesla, Einstein, Mozart, someone, who is an artist or singer now, someone in the field of business that you are interested in.

Write the words:

> Through Divine Power
>
> In A Perfect Way NOW
>
> What others have done, I can do and more
>
> I am unlimited.
>
> I can do it.

Put this where it is visual to you daily on your wall, inside a medicine cabinet, on your refrigerator, for example.

Look at it each morning and every chance you get.

Focus on the intent.

Do this until you achieve your goal.

"Faith without action is dead". Go out and work on it!

AFFIRMATION FOR MONEY

<u>Affirm</u>:

> I have millions of dollars and am now free to do the work of the God and Goddess. Thank you God. Thank you Goddess.

Reaffirm this frequently and build an emotional level of expectancy. After all, it does come in. We just might not know the time.

MONEY TO COME TO YOU

Hold a dollar bill or any folding money in your hand, so that you can read the words on it.

<u>Say</u>:

Money, money, in my hand,

Magnetize yourself.

Bring more money to me now,

Ten times 10 times 10.

So Be It!

As you spend these bills, they attract much more.

ALL PURPOSE CANDLE SPELL

Use a gold or orange candle. Carve on it:

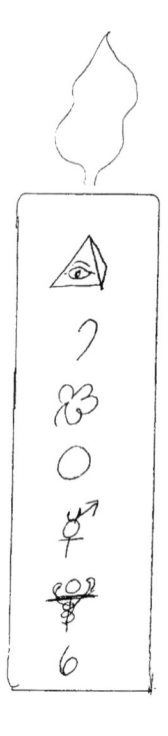

On a piece of white paper, write your intent. Place it under the candle.

Anoint the candle with High John Oil or Rose Oil.

Concentrate deeply as you work.

Light the candle.

Concentrate. The more energy and concentration, the better for success.

Let it burn out by itself.

Walk away.

The reason you will walk away in rituals is, that you know once you have done the work, it is activated and will have the outcome you worked on.

We know it works. We trust it. So there isn't a reason to look back, to question.

PROSPERITY POWER

Do this on a Thursday.

On a white candle, carve your name and:

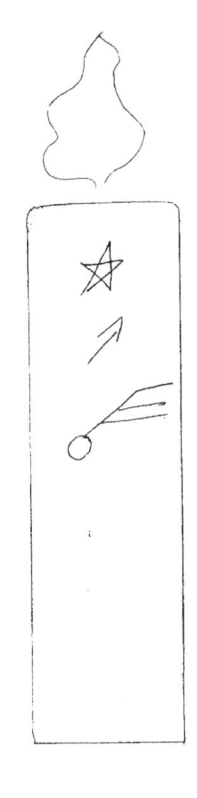

On a white paper, draw:

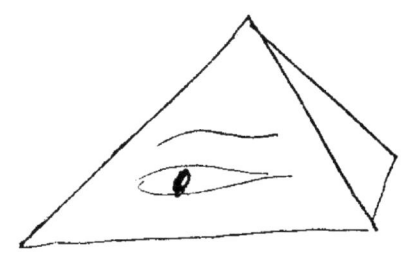

Place this under the candle

Light the candle and say:

I conjure thus:

Cerridwen, Heh, Tula, now come to my aid. Activate the Forces that be, to bring prosperity to me. In a positive way. I conjure thus:

Cerridwen, Heh, Tula!

So Mote It Be!

Let the candle burn to the bottom.

Bury it.

BLODENWEDD'S RITUAL

On a white candle, sprinkle some Alfalfa.
Set up your altar on a white cloth, facing East.

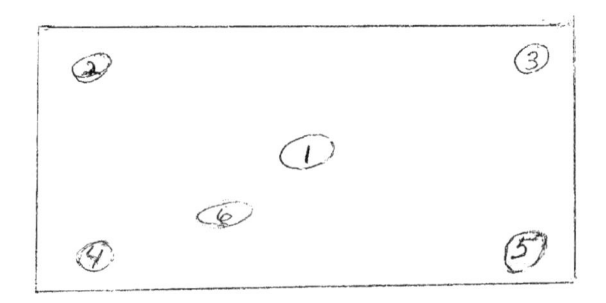

Placement:
- #1- Draw a pentagram on parchment paper. White or gold.
- #2- Place High John Incense.
- #3- Place the candle.
- #4- Place a goblet of water.
- #5- A green feather or leaf.
- #6- A clear Quartz Crystal.

Light the incense and then the candle.

Focus your thoughts before you make your petition.

Then say:

I call on Blodeuwedd. Come to my aid. Increase the prosperity in my life. Do this (fill in) for the purpose of (fill in). I n a very positive way.
Thank you Blodeuwedd. Go forth to do this NOW.

Let the candle and the incense burn out.

Keep the stone in your bedroom or place of business to prosper.

RITUAL-MONEY TO COME IN

Set the altar in this placement:

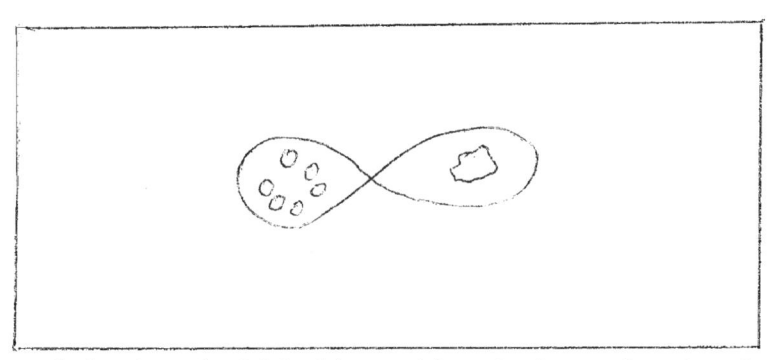

On a green cloth, place the Malachite necklace (or loose pieces) to form an infinity symbol.

Inside the left circle, place an Obsidian or 6 small pieces. In the right circle, place a Pyrite.

"Fix" the edges of the cloth with Success Oil or Money Oil.

To "Fix": focus on your intent as you put one or two drops of oil on your fingertip. Start at the top left corner and run your finger along the edge towards the right until you are back at the same spot where you began.

Leave everything on your altar until it "hits". (comes in).

AFFIRMATION

Affirm: for prosperity and abundance:

I am open to the Splendor of the Kingdom of God and a flow of plenty follows.

Give thanks to God and Blessings on and off, daily.

TO SELL PROPERTY

Get a red 7 Day Candle. Focus your goal.

Affirm:

The perfect buyer bought the house. I already sold it. I use the money from it constructively.

TO GET A JOB

Light a red Seven-Day Candle.
Put money under it. It can be a dollar.
Visualize yourself working happily.
Let the candle burn to the bottom.

MONEY AND LUCK

In the Four Corners of your room (East, West, North and South) place a bag containing money and dried Rose Petals or Rose Buds.

BUSINESS/MONEY CIRCLE

Draw a circle.

Inside the circle, place some money. The business that you will increase needs to be written on a piece of paper. Such as the type of job or a company name. Add this into the circle.

Sprinkle some Fenugreek on this.

Cut three 5-inch sticks and place them in a triangle shape on top of everything.

Leave where it is until it comes in.

MONEY PATH FOR WEALTH

Focus on money coming to you. Do not think of how it will come, just of what you can do with it. Example: buy a car, help family and others, and enjoy your life more.

Then say:

> Black is black,
> White is white,
> The path I choose,
> Is always Right.

Listen to your urges/intuition when you deal with anything connected to finance. Then move on it.

MONEY DOLL RITUAL - FOR PLAYING NUMBERS

Supplies:

Money Drawing or High John Oil

Parchment paper (or white paper)

5 green candles

5 white candles

Doll with straw sewn into it and Orris Root.

Focus your mind on the color purple for a few minutes.

Write WIN on the parchment paper 3 times. Add any number that comes to your mind or that you like to play. Attach it to the doll.

Put some of the oil on the doll and some on the parchment.

Anoint the green candles

Anoint the white candles.

Place the doll between two candles-one white, one green.

Set the other candles aside for now.

Say three times:

>Candles, candles burning bright,
>
>Bring my luck with quick reply.
>
>Through the Goddess I invoke,
>
>Luck comes to me forever more.
>
>So Be It.

Light the candles. Let them burn out on their own.

When this is done, wrap the doll in something convenient that hasn't been used for other purposes. Put it away in a safe place.

Do this every other day.

Do 5 rituals (five days of work).

Best time to do this is before you play.

MONEY AND PROSPERITY RITUAL

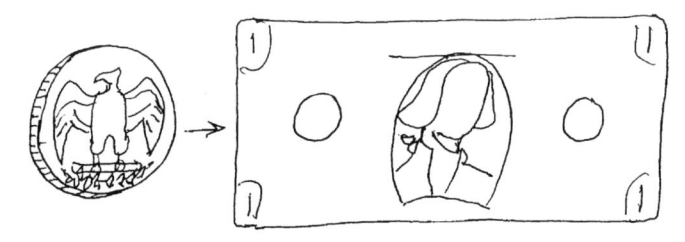

One dollar bill-face up

Silver Dollar-Eagle Head up

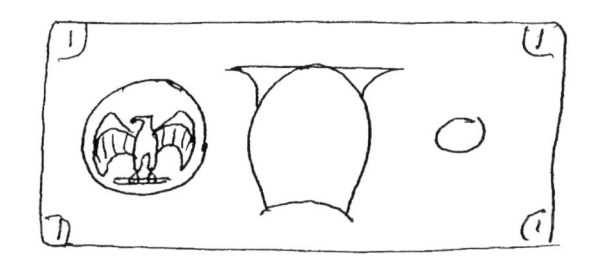

Place the quarter to the left side, on the bill.

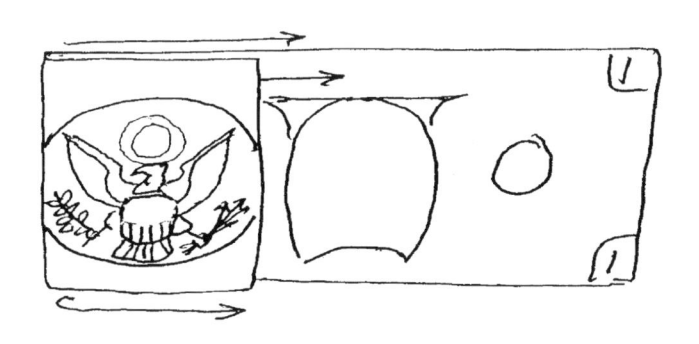

Fold, so that the Eagle side of the bill covers the quarter. As seen in diagram.

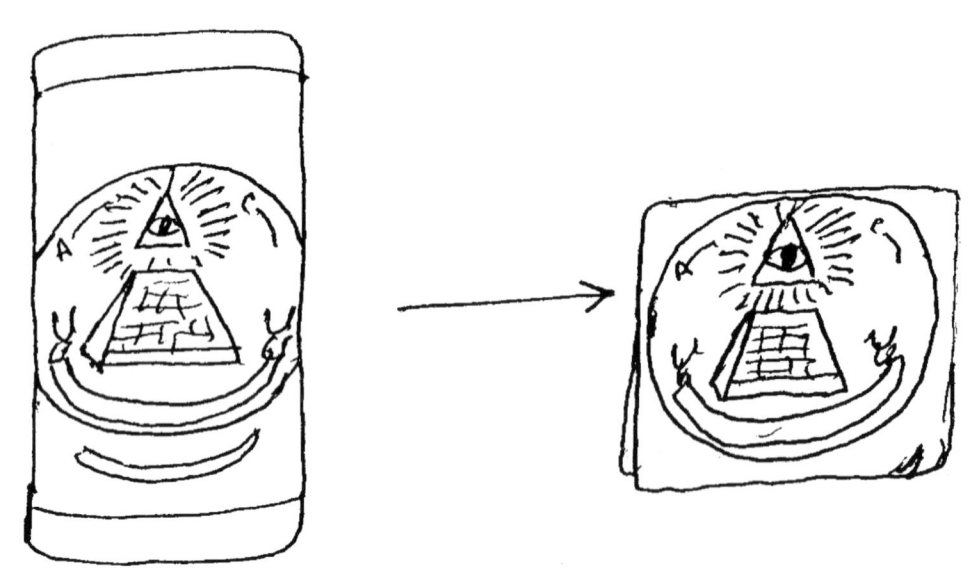

Continue to fold from left to right, so that you have the pyramid side of the bill shown on top

Now, fold the top down and bottom up, so that it is compacted

Secure with clear tape.

Anoint it with Success, Money or Prosperity Oil.

Place it into a green pouch.

Add a few Sage Leaves and a little Chamomile.

Add eight drops of the oil into the pouch.

Carry this with you.

CHAPTER EIGHT

A
HEALTHY
LIFE
EQUALS
A
BALANCED
LIFE

Healers have been with us since ancient times. Called by many names such as Magi, Shaman, Wiccan, Sorcerer, Witch Doctor and Medicine Man.

Long before we had modern medicine, which is the baby of the medical field, we had other methods and still do.

Acupuncture, herbs, spiritual healings, laying on of hands, words-of-power, elixirs, to name just a few.

These methods work or they would not have lasted through centuries to this day.

We always recommend that you use whatever method feels right to you. After all, we are all different. These methods are not meant as a replacement for the medical field. All fields of health care are positive,

Wiccans do not practice one form of healing, but are open to different systems. Many times they will use one system for a burn and another system for a different problem.

Due to the attitude of openness, of non-prejudice, they are unlimited in finding the correct cure for each problem.

Herbs and stones were always utilized. When carried or worn on the body or within three feet, they were known to work. They have their own vibrational effects (as scientifically shown now).

You do not need to add your belief system to activate their energies. Although in some rituals, there are other methods, including belief, to add and heighten the forces already present.

There are numerous methods for healing.

These are ancient tools for modern man.

EXCESS WATER

When your body is holding too much water, take Sage and Parsley frequently to take it out.

CUTS AND BRUISES

Rub Wolfbane on these areas for relief. Wolfbane is also good for arthritis and achy muscles.

It can be found in many martial arts stores and pharmacies under the name of Arnica.

HEIGHTEN ABILITY TO HEAL

To speed up your natural healing process, keep a Chrysanthemum plant (live-not cuttings or dried) near you. Good in a hospital room or your bedroom.

Cuts your healing time in half.

Ask the Goddess Diana for help in the healing process. Then thank her.

GOLD POWER TO HEAL

On a gold candle, carve:

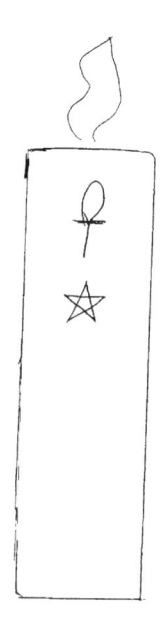

Then add your name.

Place a gold colored Topaz within one inch.

Sprinkle some gold sparkles on the candle top.

Light it and say:

> I invoke the Master of Healing to help me and to stay with me until the work is done, in a positive way.
> I know that as I ask, I am already in the process of healing.

So Mote It Be!

You will then let the candle burn down on its own.
When this is done, throw the remaining wax out to the wind.

Then pick up the stone and wear it on your body until healed. Wear it at all times. At night, wear it or place it within 3 feet of your body.

For the purpose of:

    Detoxing

    Digestive system

    Tissue regeneration

    Liver

    Spleen

THE VISION OF GNOMES

Set your altar up as follows:

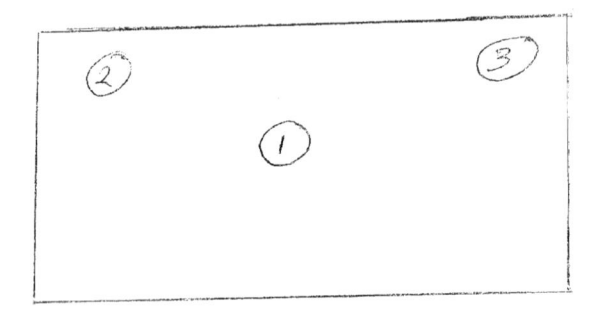

Place:

    # 1- Opal

    # 2- Green candle

    # 3- Pink candle

Light the candles and say:

Gnomes of the Inner Earth, come now to my aid.

Improve my eyesight 100 fold. Improve my vision.

Gnomes of the Earth, hear me! I call you forth. Stay until my eyesight improves. Thank you. Blessed Be.

> So Be It.

Let the candles burn out. Bury them.
Carry the stone on your body at all times. You can even wear it as jewelry.

BACKACHE PREVENTION

In a green or pink bag, carry Mugwort near your body.

BENEFICIAL NUTRIENTS

For your body to get the most from nutrients, get a Fluorite stone. Hold it in your hand and <u>say</u>:

Fluorite with your special color,

Healing energies now heighten.

I call upon Apollo's aid,

This stone I now consecrate!

<u>For the purpose of:</u>

Aiding the physical body to get the most nutrients.

Thank you, Apollo.

So Be It.

Carry the stone at all times.

TO BANISH PAIN

Do not confuse not having pain with not having a problem or that you are cured.

It simply stops or tones down the pain so you can deal better.

It does NOT heal.

Two formulae:

> # 1- Visualize yourself with orange light-the shade of the spectrum surrounding the painful area or the whole body. Keep your focus on the orange light for 15-20 minutes the most.

> # 2- Get an orange light bulb-the color of the spectrum-and sit under the light. Have it shine on the problem area or your whole body. Do this for no more then 15-20 minutes.

You can set a kitchen timer, as an example, so your focus does not leave the color, or so that when you get involved in T.V. or a book, you will not lose track of the time.

You can do this more then once per day.

However, not for more then 15-20 minutes at a time.

If you overdo, you will off balance your system. This could cause an other problem.

HEALING SEA SPELL

Take a piece of coral in your hand.

Say:

Coral of the deepest sea,

I call Poseidon now to me.

Healing energy now freely flows,

From Sea God to this Coral I hold.

As I will,

So Shall It Be.

Thank you now,

God of the Sea.

Carry it at all times.

Each day, hold the Coral in your hands for five minutes.

Close your eyes. Relax. Take 3 deep breaths.

See yourself in Perfect health, with a happy smile.

Feel or know the Corals energy is flowing into you.

You may feel warmth, coolness, or a tingling sensation.

THROAT PROBLEMS-OR PAINFUL AREAS

Place your fingertips on that area, say:

Divine Love is healing me now. I love myself (fill in your name).

> I call in the God and Goddess to help me heal quickly, easily now. Stay with me until I completely heal. I allow myself to heal. I love myself. My body now is healing.

Repeat this on and off.

CURE DEPRESSION-AVOID FEVER

Wear St. John's Wort next to your skin to cure your depression and prevent fevers. Place the St. John's Wort in front of you and <u>invoke</u>:

> I call upon you, Baldur! Light my way so I heal-
> <u>(pick one or both intents)</u>.
> Do this for me NOW. Do this through your Power and through this St. John's Wort.
> Do this until it is completed.
> Thank you Baldur!

Then wear it.

ILLNESS PREVENTION

Carry the blossoms of the Wind Flower. Also called Anemone.

Place them in a pink bag.

Prevention is always best.

If you can not find this flower, good substitutes are Ginger and Low John The Conqueror.

TOBACCO-DIGESTION AID

Smoking natural tobacco or chewing on the leaf helps if you are having a digestion problem.

Burn Tobacco Incense to purify the area you sleep in.

Call on the help of the Green Man (A God).

METABOLISM

Chew on about a pinch of Chinese Black Sesame Seeds.

This is a multi-purpose use:

>Evens out the sugar in your metabolism

>Curbs your appetite

>Helps you to stop smoking

RED STRENGTH

To vitalize your bloodstream, do the following formula:

Hold a red Garnet in your hand

Sprinkle some Peppermint on it.

Say:

> I call on the Power of the earth. Energize this stone.
>
> I call on the Power of Brigid. Activate this stone.
>
> I call on the Power of Appolo. Increase the Power of this stone.
>
> So Mote It Be.

The forces are already in the stone. This ritual heightens them,

Throw the herbs to the wind.

Carry the stone.

IMMUNE SYSTEM

To improve your immune system, use the following herbs by themselves or in any combination.

>Garlic
>
>Licorice Root
>
>Bulga Weed
>
>Planters Leaves

ELFIN NECKLACE

Wear a neck lace made of Jasper to keep you healthy and to recuperate much faster then you would normally.

MOON HEALING

Place your altar so the moonlight shines on it or outdoors. The time of the night does not matter.

Place some Gardenia on your altar with the name of the ill person or a picture of him/her next to it.

Burn Gardenia Incense.

Ask for the favor of the Gods. Then ask for the help of The Triple Goddess for the purpose of (fill in) for (fill in the name), to be done NOW. Then thank them for their help.

Let the incense burn out and with the Gardenia, bury the picture or name next to the roots of any growing tree or plant.

Make sure the plant is not sick or place it near a new plant.

HOUSE OF HEALING

If you are ill at home or in a hospital room, scatter some Gardenia around the floor. It will speed up your healing process.

THE SPELL OF IVY

Plant some Ivy near your home so that the leaves are readily available to you. Ivy can be added to any healing ritual.

MEDICINE BAG-HEALING

In a green pouch, add:

> Chrysanthemum
>
> Gardenia
>
> Bay
>
> Mugwort
>
> Carnation
>
> Turquoise-stone
>
> And a White paper with your petition for health written on it.

Close the bag with three knots.
Carry it next to your body at all times.

MERCURY'S TREE

Take any part of the Willow Tree to burn. Ask the tree for permission first. If you do not have any negative feelings, use this tree.

In a cauldron or a container that you can burn this in, place the Willow.

On a piece of paper, write your petition. Put this on top, then add a little more Willow on the paper.

Light it. Relight it when necessary until the whole paper is ashes.

As it burns, focus on your intent.

When it has burned to ashes, throw all of the mixture to the winds.

STONE OF HEALING

On a piece of Jasper that you will be able to wear or carry, inscribe the following:

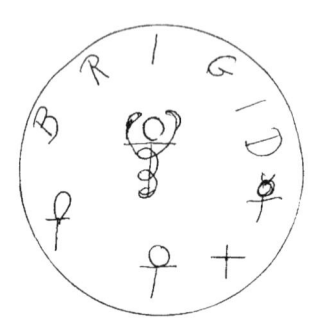

Sprinkle some Thyme on it.

Focus on your intent- as this being a Healing Stone that is activated.

Throw the Thyme to the winds.

Carry the stone.

If you choose, you can carry it in a green bag.

You can coat it with clear nail polish or something clear. This way, the Sigils will stay on longer. Only coat it on the Sigils, not on the rest of the stone.

ALTAR WORK

On an altar, place:

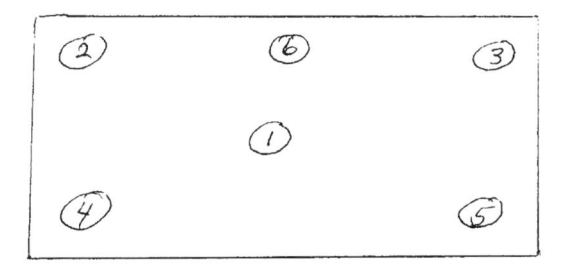

[Diagram: rectangle with positions labeled 2 (top-left), 6 (top-center), 3 (top-right), 1 (center), 4 (bottom-left), 5 (bottom-right)]

As follows:

1- Turquoise

2- Green Candle

3 –White Candle

4- Violet

5- Fennel

6 – Pink Candle

Light the candles in the order that you put them out, with a clear purpose for healing. Ask for the aid of Artemis in your healing work, until it is completed. Say thank you.

Let the candles burn to the bottom. Then throw them away-what remains-outside your home or work area.

Carry the herbs and the stone in a green pouch.

ONION SPELLS

1- Take an onion and cut it in half. Rub it on the part of your body where there is illness.

Visualize all the illness going into it.

Bury it.

#2- Hang a red onion above your bed to protect against illness and to help recuperate. If you are ill, focus the illness going into the onion. When you have healed fully, throw the onion away outside and place a new one in its place.

#3- Write the name of the ill person on a piece of paper. Wrap it around the onion. Bury it.

PEPPER SPELL

You need branches of the Pepper Tree. Take a few and brush the ill person with them.

This absorbs the illness.

Bury all the branches to eliminate the illness from the body.

HEALTH TALISMAN

On a cord, ribbon or thread, which is green or white, strings the following stones:

Amber

Calcite

Carnelian

Jasper

Emerald

Jade

You can usually find the stones to string in a Lapidary (Rock Shop), hobby shop or craft store.

Wear or carry this at all times.

You can wear it as a necklace or on a short string, put it in your pocket.

Carry it within three feet of your body.

SLEEP AID

Prior to going to bed, drink a few teacups of Chrysanthemum tea.

Put some Chrysanthemum leaves near your bed.

PEACEFUL SLEEP

Make a small square from cotton material, or material that has an open weave.

Fill it with Lavender and place it between the pillow and the pillowcase

HEALING CANDLE

On a green candle, carve the name of the ill person and the following:

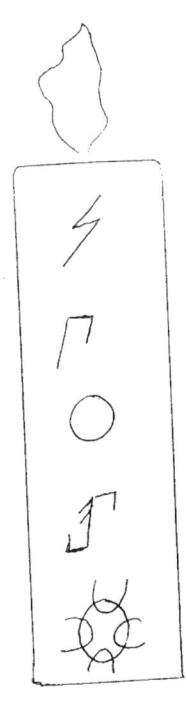

Sprinkle Thyme at the base.

Focus on your petition as you write it down.

Write the person's name on it. Add what the illness is or write-for Perfect Health.

Place it under the candle.

Light it and focus on your petition for 5 minutes.

Let it burn to the bottom.

Bury it.

HEALING ELIXIR

Take a clear glass with water and add Jasper. Wash it first.

Let it sit in direct sunlight for a day.

Take the stone out and drink it.

Repeat the process until you are better.

ACORN SPELL

On a piece of paper, write:

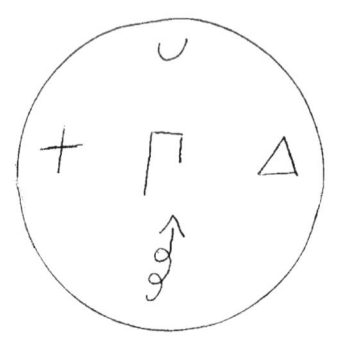

Take an acorn from an Oak Tree and wrap it in the paper.

Hold it in your hand and focus on what your outcome is or petition for Perfect Health.

Take the acorn and bury it beneath an Oak Tree.

Walk away and do not look back.

DISTANT HEALING

You, as the healer, stand behind an empty chair.

Envision the ill person sitting in the chair. (Put the person mentally in the chair). You are putting their essence in.

Then focus on White Light coming from above you, out through your fingers as Healing Energy and send it to the image in the chair.

When you are done, put your hands under running water. (Like a faucet or stream).

SEA MAGIC FOR HEALTH

Use damp sand to form into the shape of a doll.

Focus on healing and your name (or the ill person's name).

Then let it be washed out to sea to carry the energy on every wave.

This method is very effective to wear down an illness.

When it is dry, you can also hold it in your hand, focus on your needs and release it to the wind and water to transport your desire.

CHAPTER NINE

DIVINING LIFE'S PURPOSES WITH POSITIVE MAGICK

Divination has been with us for centuries.

There are numerous methods to be utilized.

Try different ones to see what you like, then make up your own rituals.

Any time that you "feel" something is not correct or you get a different urge, go by it. Your intuition, your psychic input always outweighs "learned" information

We live in both realities. The physical and the non-physical. You need both to attain balance.

The seeker needs to look within, where all the answers lie.

These divination tools and rituals are meant to aid and to reawaken your own natural abilities and intuitive knowledge.

Psychic information is not set in stone. We, as psychics see the Path that is automatically coming up for you if you continue your life just as you are.

Remember that we have free will!

When you receive positive information, simply continue as you have been.

When you receive negative information, you will need to make a <u>conscious</u> choice.

You can keep going along the same path and have the situation occur. Or you can change it. You can avoid it or at least improve the situation.

Divination is meant to guide you. Not to tell you what to do.

It is a tool that can greatly improve your life. Work with it and remember you have choices to make on your Path of Life. Make the right ones for you.

YES/NO CARD SPREAD

Take playing cards and shuffle the deck.

Concentrate clearly on your question. Phrase it so the answer would be yes or no.

Shuffle as long as you feel. When you stop, pick three cards from the top.

Lay them face up in front of you.

If most of the cards are red, the answer is-Yes.

If most of the cards are black, the answer is-No.

Once you have your answer, do not ask the same question again in any form.

WATER DIVINATION

Fill a bowl with water. Make sure the bowl does not have any designs on the inside.

Place the bowl on a black surface, such as a cloth or paper.

Dim the lights in the room or simply make sure there aren't any distractions.

Sit comfortably in front of the bowl.

Stare into it. Pick one place in the bowl to stare into.

You will find, this helps you un-focus your vision faster.

If you have a question, ask it now. It can be on any subject.

You may repeat the question if needed.

Be open to any form that the answer comes to you in. As an example; you may "see" an image that makes sense to you; you may "see" one that you will need to make sense of later; you may get a feeling what to do or how someone feels about you; you may get a great idea; just "know" all of a sudden or you may not receive anything. Then a day later you'll "realize" what the answer is. This is not a separate situation. The psychic information was triggered by the water ritual.

When you are finished, throw the water out outside your house.

DIVINATION FOR LUCKY NUMBERS

This is a system for a 52-card deck.

Aces=1, numbers 2-10, place the Jokers aside, place the court cards aside.

Steps:

1)- Shuffle the cards 9 to 10 times or when you feel the need to stop.

2)- Split the deck into 3 piles. From left to right.

3)- Restack from right to left by skipping the middle stack and placing it on top of the other two.

4)- Draw 3 cards per one set of 3 digit numbers.

5)- Draw 4 cards per one set of 4 digit numbers.

6)- Draw 6 cards per one set of 6 digit numbers.

If you want to place any lotto game that has numbers from 11-80.

Step:

1)- Follow step # 6 and for each number between 1-10 multiply by 4 for one column and for any additional numbers add or subtract any key number you pick.

Example:

Using step # 6=1,8,10,4,7,9 multiply by 4=4,32,40,16,28,36

2)- now you select your favorite key number.

Example:

7 then add/or subtract your key number to/from Row # 2

Step # 6)-   1, 8, 10, 4, 7, 9   Row 1
(x 4)- 4, 32, 40, 16, 28, 36   Row 2
(+) - 11,39,47, 23, 35, 43   Row 3
(-) - 3, 25, 33, 9, 21, 29   Row 4

Now you have a nice batch of numbers to select from. Which will leave you room to experiment.

PSYCHOMETRY

WHAT OS PSYCHOMETRY? - Psychometry is a word that was coined in 1842 to express a new science and art. It comes from two Greek words: psych (soul) and metro (measure). Today, it has taken on the meaning of receiving psychic impressions from an object by way of holding it in their hands.

HOW DOES PSYCHOMETRY WORK? – There are two parts to the mechanics of this science:

1. All objects become influenced by an individual's or an environment's magnetism as the object's aura absorbs the vibrations.
2. The human (and animal) skin contains a number of light-sensitive cells called PHOTO SENSITIVE CELLS. These cells are concentrated in the skin on the hands and on the back.

So by putting these two factors together, a sensitive is able to receive the impression of the object.

A. A good trance medium can get in touch with a recently departed soul by holding an object from that person.

B. It should be noted that psychometry should not be confined to the holding of objects only. There are also forms of psychometry that involve the feeling or hearing of voice vibrations in a room.

C. Vibrations can also be seen. For example: A woman fell asleep on a bus going cross-country. When the bus had made a rest stop, all of the passengers had gotten off except her. She woke up when all the passengers were still off the bus but could see the vibrations of the passengers just as if they were sitting in their seats.

D. Visions may come to you in small or large pictures. Visions may come to you fast or slow. The person who is receiving the impressions may take on the characteristics of the owner of the object.

ALWAYS WASH YOUR HANDS AFTER!

A. WHEN.

B. When doing a reading for someone, ask"When will this event take place"? Ask for a time, day, month and year.

C. You can use this question to predict future happenings, such as earth changes (earthquakes, volcanic eruptions, floods, etc.).

D. WHERE

E. Where did this object come from?

F. Where did the owner live?

G. (Doing a reading) Where did the owner loose another object?

H. HOW

I. How was this object used?

J. A friend of mine is occasionally asked to help the police and is given an object, asking how did a certain crime happen.

K. WHO

L. Who used this object?

M. Who was involved in the crime? (Ask for a name).

N. WHAT (most important question to be asked)

O. What is this object?

P. What will the outcome of a certain event be?

Q. What is around the object?

R. WHY

   1. Why did this event take place? What lesson is to be learned through this experience?

You can preserve the vibrations of an object by placing them in a thin rubber cloth.

EXERCISES FOR DEVELOPING SENSITIVITY FOR PSYCHOMETRY

1. Use a bowl of water that is body temperature. Without looking, lower your fingers until they are just above the water level. (many times a person will contact the water first).
2. Place a penny, nickel, dime and quarter in the hand without looking and see what kind of taste develops in your mouth.
3. Place either salt or sugar in your hand and see what kind of taste develops in your mouth.
4. Place colors face down in the palm of the hand and verbalize what kind of sensations are received: cool, hot, calm, anger, light, etc.

ESTABLISHING CONNECTIONS WITH THE GOD/GODDESS

Select the appropriate colored candle for each and place them on a table or altar in the following cardinal positions: East, South, West, North.

Use Frankincense as the incense.

Encircle yourself with White Light. Then, as you light each candle invoke the name of the God/Goddess of each direction three times.

Next, light the incense and sit in silence with your heart and mind open and aware to any impressions seen and/or felt.

Take at least an hour.

Journal the experience.

Be aware of the type of dreams you will have and record them so they can be analyzed.

Transfer all notes into your Book of Shadows or keep it in a special notebook.

You can do this once a week, twice or once a month.

By doing this, you can review, evaluate and observe your growth.

DREAM WORK

To gain information through a dream, make an elixir.

Take a Lapis Lazuli stone and place it in a clear glass filled with water.

Keep it in direct sunlight for a day.

Take the stone out and drink the water before going to bed.

At the time you go to sleep, place the Lapis Lazuli under your pillowcase.

Ask your question three times. Go to sleep.

Put a pen and paper next to your bed. Upon awakening, write down everything you remember. You can take your time to look at it at any time.

You will have very vivid dreams.

If you do not get an answer by the time you wake up, repeat the ritual. You will get an answer between 1-3 nights.

Ask for the dream to be understandable for you.

FIRE SCRYING

Build a campfire or if you have a fireplace, use that.

Once the flames are high, stare into the flame.

Ask your question and let your vision unfocus as you stare.

Ask for the aid of the Fire Drakes. Thank them when you are finished.

As you look into the flames, pay attention to anything you see in them, pictures or symbols. Also, you need to be aware of what you feel or sense.

You might get an idea you did not have before.

Do not repeat the same question if you were not answered. Wait. Then repeat it on a different day.

CHAPTER TEN

HOW TO FAX YOUR HEART'S DESIRES – THROUGH MEDITATION AND VISUALIZATION

Meditation is one of the most well known, but least understood methods of self-awareness. There are numerous forms passed down through the ages. However, some forms are not really workable. They are impressive to the uninitiated.

If you read a book and it gives you a method which sounds very difficult, but the author (teacher, guru, etc)'looks as though he can perform it and you cannot---then do NOT work with it.

First, it is not for you. Secondly, in most cases, it is not the real method employed by the teacher. It just makes the teacher look more impressive (he is working on his own ego or finance).

The most effective methods I find are ancient ones. They are simple and direct. Thus, full power.

In ancient times they needed to tune in fast. They did not have the time to waste on trying to be dramatic. They needed to use their time for (unimportant pursuits), survival.

Meditation is a method to go "within" yourself. To tune into the Godhead within you. It is your link to Divine Power.

Any method, which is external, is working against yourself. First you need to tune the external out prior going within.

When you tune in to information through meditation, you block out your outside awareness first.

After all, you are going to shift from one reality (the physical/material), to the other reality (spiritual/ astral). Both are equally real.

To go within, you need to disassociate from the physical reality.

During meditation, you are on a psychic level. Scientists have tested the brain waves during meditation.(During psychic awareness).

They have found that when we are working from this, our everyday reality, our brainwaves are on a Beta level. This is the same as when we converse with each other, do our work, go shopping, or whatever our daily lives include.

When on a psychic level (meditation included), it is tested as being on Alpha and Theta. I tell people it is as though you are on an Alpha High.(You are really on Alpha/Theta waves).

The external methods you need to reject are the ones where you focus on candles, music, colors, anything outside.

These methods are good before or after meditation if you enjoy them

As an example: If you like music, you can listen to it prior to starting. This can be helpful to you as a form of relaxation.

These forms are really teaching you concentration, not meditation!

Visualization is deliberately bringing a desire into manifestation.

You do this by picturing the desire in your mind.

Your focus is on the end result.

The picture will become a strong enough thought, to form into physical reality.

Example of how manifestation works:

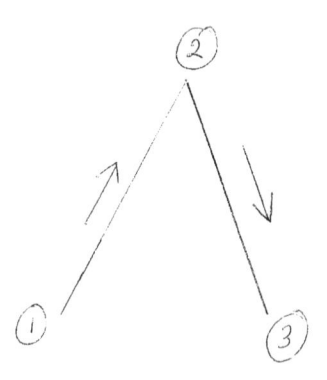

1- You first have the thought. After all, remember that there is power in the word/thought.

2- It goes to the astral reality to form.

3- It comes down to manifest in the physical world.

You need to keep your mind clear to be able to focus,

Do not cloud your thinking by what can or can not be attained.

Thought forms are real. Out mind gives them direction on what to do.

Be clear and precise on what you want as the end result, so it can build on the etheric plane.

This is why repeated sessions make it better.

You can use visualization for yourself or for others

The purpose is unlimited. Love, friendship, health, wealth or whatever you desire.

Visualization is a key.

Success is not something you do. First it is something you thought.

Once you are definite-you will be at the right place, right time, right people, everything will just fall into place.

An occult saying is that everything follows thought.

We live in a holographic universe and create our own realities by thought.

At this point, even some scientists think that both matter and space exists due to human thought.

Scientists and metaphysicians believe the same, just express it differently. Quantum reality is what Magis' know.

The mind is the creator of our universe, our reality.

Some masters of yoga can create physical objects by developing their consciousness to such a high state.

Symbols, rituals, colors, among other things like visualization, are to bring your desires about.

When you look at Wiccan beliefs, you will realize, as with all belief systems, they have been using this knowledge all along.

To help themselves have better lives, to help others, to help the community, animals, plants, the earth in general.

When looking at meditation and visualization, remember, one is passive, the other active. Rather, Meditation is information.

Visualization is attention, which is energy.

ALPHA REALITY

There are levels of awareness that we can consciously put to use.

Beta – which is our normal, everyday brainwave level. Alpha & Theta – which is where psychic occurrences happen. And Delta.

These are altered states of awareness. It is a though you were seeing two realities. Both equally real. One is this material reality and the other Alpha reality. It is merely an ability to tune in.

The average person only uses 10 % of his potential. With your brainwave on Alpha, you can heighten this level and put it to use to help yourself and others.

First you need to learn how to relax your body and mind. To block out sensory impulses to develop your subconscious. And to develop super-awareness.

You need to block out your mental thought process. You can not do two things at the same time. If you are thinking, you can not go down to deeper levels within yourself. Just as you can not if your legs are cramped, since your thoughts will then be centered in that direction.

One of the most effective ways to tune into Alpha, is to meditate. First visualize and feel yourself inside each color of the rainbow. (Red, Orange, Yellow, Green, Blue, Violet).And with each color go deeper into yourself. Then slowly count backwards from 20-1. Feeling more and more relaxed and going deeper. When you get to 1, visualize a door in front of you. Go through it and into a comfortable room with a big white screen.

Here is where you will see what is in your past, present and future. If you need to solve a problem, as an example, you would put the problem on your screen and give it a little time to give you a way to solve it. The answer will come to you.

There is the Infinity of the Universe in all of us, and so we are all connected. Tuned in. When you go down into your levels, you acquire the ability to create, heal, understand, etc. If you want to reorganize your negative habits, you visualize it in a positive way on the screen. Your subconscious sees both as reality (Beta & Alpha). It also takes everything literally. Through visualization and meditation, it will accept your input and change your life outwardly. Your body and consciousness will respond fast.

We are responsible for our thoughts, which cause these changes. Remember:-"Ask & ye shall receive, seek & ye shall find, knock & the door shall be opened". This is a very real way of working with your life.

Alpha solves problems after your consciousness says-" I give up! Help!" It balances you physically, mentally and emotionally.

It is a positive way to acquire what you want or need and to help others.

As Emerson said-" Be careful of what you wish for, or you may get it". With practice, you will go into Alpha faster. Work with it and be constructive.

VISUALIZATION FOR ANY DESIRE

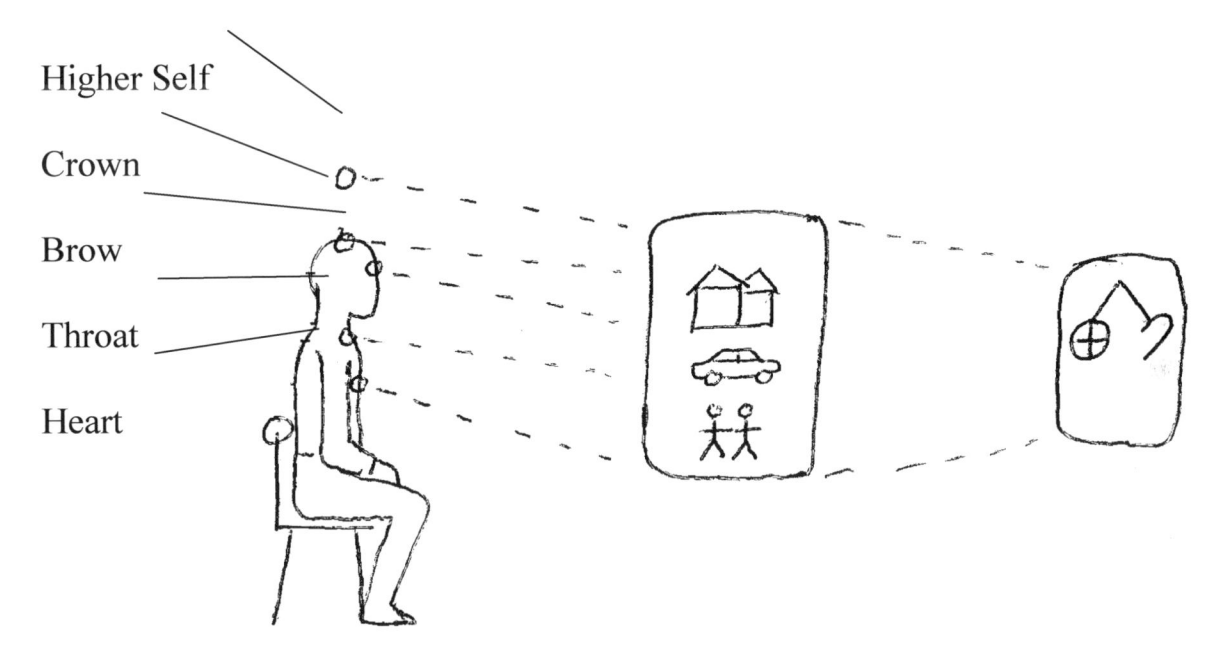

- Higher Self
- Crown
- Brow
- Throat
- Heart

You are working with five of the Chakras. The <u>Higher Self</u> is your connection with the Divine. The <u>Crown</u> is manifestation of Divinity. The <u>Brow</u> is activated to visualize. The <u>Throat</u> is for Power of the Word. The <u>Heart</u> is the Divine in you.

Sit with your spine aligned so you are sitting straight.

Close your eyes if you are newer or more comfortable-to visualize better.

Picture your idea(s) of what you want into colors or symbols with an affirmation. (A statement of what you want). You can "see" a house, a new car and a relationship. Sense it, feel it, see it, then "Download" it to a picture in front of you.

Or the second way to visualize, is with colors with a symbol(s) in place of actual pictures. Think of a symbol(s) that to you, represents what you want. As an example, in this situation you can draw a rooftop for the house, a circle with a cross in it's center to represent the steering wheel of the car and the right half of a heart. Now put these into one symbol. You will be the only one who knows what you visualize, so make it a form you like.

Once you form this in your mind and project it in font of you, picture energy flowing into it from your five Chakras for a minute or two.

When you are done, slowly open your eyes, knowing your manifestation will come in, then walk away. Go do other things. You only need to do this once.

MEDITATION TO GAIN INFORMATION

Sit comfortably on a chair.

Close your eyes and relax.

Relax your body, relax your mind.

Take three slow breaths to relax your muscles.

Picture a warm summer day in a comfortable setting.

Let yourself feel the peace and the sacred space around you.

Say to yourself:

I am on sacred ground. I am safe and serene.

Mentally wrap yourself in White Light.

MAGICKAL MEDITATION

To learn magick to be able to create anything you want.

This meditation will give you the ability to gain direct knowledge from the astral plane on how to manifest your desire.

Sit comfortably with your spine straight.

Close your eyes and take three deep breaths, slowly.

Picture this Sigil in front of you for as long as you can. At least a minute.

You can also picture the Sigil without the circle.

Focus on the name Milon.

Say:

> I now call in Milon, in a positive way,
>
> Through Divine Power. I petition you to give me
>
> information on how to create magickally anything I
>
> choose.

Then just relax. Do not focus on anything.

Pay attention to anything you 'see", "feel" or just "know", or ideas that come to you.

When you are done, open your eyes slowly.

Pay attention to any ideas you have in the next few days.

Make sure you thank Milon, and say- **Go forth!**

You can get up and resume your daily activities.

VISUALIZATION TO RECHARGE

To recharge your energy, stand with your feet apart at shoulder length.

Arms comfortably at your sides. Hands relaxed.

Breathe in for a count of three slowly.

Hold the breath for a count of three.

Breathe out for a count of three.

As you breathe in, visualize cosmic energy as white light flowing into your body and recharging it.

Storing the energy.

As you breathe out, send the energy flow out through your hands.

Repeat the cycle a few times.

Focus your mind on the question you want to ask

Visualize a large TV or movie screen in front of you and a little above your eye level, in gold.

Ask your focused question.

Wait for the answer and "look" at the screen.

If you have other thoughts come in which you know are not related to your question (bills, problems, positive "other" things), simply acknowledge them and say- **I am now waiting for my answer.** Then look at the screen again.

When you are finished, take one deep breath and slowly open your eyes.

TO IMPROVE A SITUATION

Sit or lay down comfortably.

Close your eyes and breathe deeply.

Visualize:

"See" an outcome for your situation. Clearly. As vividly as you can.

Take your time. Add as many details as possible.

Then say:

I am the daughter/son of the God and Goddess, all obstacles fall away.

My (fill in the situation) is exactly as I see it and know it to be.

When you are done, slowly open your eyes.

Walk away and do not focus on it again in your every day thinking. Do not question the results.

VISUALIZATION FOR A MAGICKAL WORK SPACE

Stand before your altar or place of work.

Visualize the area peaceful and surrounded by White Light.

Say:

> The ground I stand on is sacred ground. The area I work in is sacred ground. I now am in a place where all is sacred, all conditions for my work are perfect.

"See" yourself finished with your work, with a smile for what you accomplished successfully.

Now you can begin your work.

GOAL VISUALIZATION

This is excellent for any goal, especially for business. Such as getting a raise, people/boss being happy with you and your work, winning a trophy.

Close your eyes. Relax.

Visualize yourself standing at the sea. On the other shore, you can see your goal.

The water is all the obstacles between you and your goal.

See the water clearly. See the color, feel the spray on your face, smell the sea.

Now, step into the water.

As you do so, see the sea open a path to you, to your goal. Watch it part!

See the dry land between the walls of water.

You feel safe and protected by the walls.

Comfortably, at a pace you pick, walk to your goal.

Step on the other shore and become part of the picture of your achieved goal.

As you take your first step into the water, say with trust:

> The waters of the Red Sea part as I go forward to my promised goal.

When you are finished, open your eyes.

FINDING YOUR DIRECTION

This meditation will help you to find what path you should take next in life, or when deciding between more then one direction.

Sit with your spine aligned.

Close your eyes and take three deep, slow breaths.

Visualize a large white or golden white screen in front of you, and a little above eye level.

See different dirt roads (paths) ahead of you. All starting, from the same point, leading in various directions.

See the roads go over a hill, so that you can not see where they lead.

Stand at the beginning, where the roads come together.

Say:

> I am led by the Divine Forces. I follow the Right path automatically. God makes a way, where the Right path leads.

Then relax, allow the information to come to you. Do not focus.

Pay attention to any urges, thoughts, feelings, any form of information you receive.

When you are done, open your eyes and write down any information you received, to be looked at later.

Pay attention for the next few days of any form of information which could be connected.

CANDLE RITUAL FOR VISUALIZATION

On a white candle, carve:

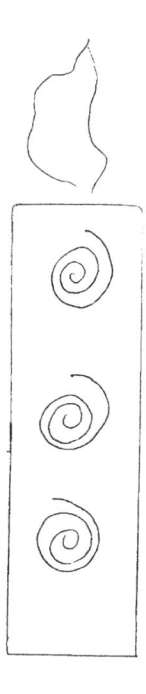

Also carve the outcome (picture or words) of what you want.

Put the candle so that it is at a convenient level to stare at the flame.

Sit comfortably, light the candle and look into the flame.

Notice how it moves back and forth.

How it moves up and down.

How it flickers.

Look at the color of the flame. Then look at the colors within the colors; white, blue.

Feel the warmth.

Now focus your mind on your intent.

See it vividly, clearly.

Put the picture into the flame. Fire is an activating force.

See is as clearly as possible.

When you are done, walk away.

Let the candle burn to the bottom.

TO CHANGE YOURSELF

This visualization is good for all purposes. Such as gaining confidence, shedding weight, becoming less shy. Whatever you would change to improve your life, to feel better about yourself.

This is strictly for you. Not because someone else wants you to be different.

Sit in a place where you will not be disturbed. Outdoors if possible.

Take a deep breath to relax.

(As an example, we will work on being a good Speaker). See the situation you pick in detail.

Visualize yourself dressed in something that fits the occasion and that you are comfortable in.

See yourself with a smile because you know the subject you will speak on.

Visualize someone talking to you before the time you will speak. You talk comfortably, it is a friendly conversation. You laugh together.

Now it is time for you and you are introduced.

You feel relaxed.

You feel good, knowing you are giving information that would be of help to others. They will be happy to have this knowledge and they will appreciate it.

You are speaking not _to_ them, but _for_ them.

Walk to where you will speak. Smile.

See yourself happy doing this.

See yourself finished and happy, comfortable and feeling like you would like to do this again to help more people. Or just happy you did this time.

Open your eyes.

Repeat this on and off until you have done what you set out to do.

It is fun reaching a goal.

While you visualize, you can also add-

This is working!

I am becoming (fill in). Example: a great speaker

(120 lbs.; confident; energetic).

OAK TREE MEDITATION

As you sit in a comfortable position, make sure your back is straight.

Close your eyes and relax.

See a picture of yourself in a forest in warm sunshine.

You are wearing something comfortable, enjoying a slight breeze.

As you walk, you see an oak tree. It is tall and strong and there is a perfect spot for you to sit, on the ground with your back leaning against the tree.

As you sit here, you think how nice it would be to meet some of the animals that live here.

You close your eyes, leaning against the tree.

You open them to see the animals.

At this point, stop visualizing.

Relax. Let any thought or picture come into your mind. Do not force it. Do not think, just relax.

When you are finished, open your eyes.

Any animal that you saw is your totem. You are able to use its qualities when you need to.

It will come to you when you call.

HOW TO RELATE TO TREES

It is important to develop a deeper understanding of nature and the earth. There are many methods and one of them is the use of meditation, along with visualization. Through meditation and visualization one can develop and receive information that links you with a multitude of essences that connect you with the elemental and spiritual nature of the earth.

A simple and basic exercise would be to first locate a tree that you can directly touch, see and smell. You want to be able to analyze and experience the subject matter mainly through these three senses and mentally record your findings by storing it away into your memory.

The next level would be your ability to recall from memory the visual aspect of the same tree by picturing it with as much detail as possible (i.e. height, width, color, texture). The more you focus on the visual details, the more the memory of the experience is brought to life within you.

Now you will need to place your emotional, psychic and empathetic nature in touch with subtle energies of the tree. This would be its own auric field of magnetism. If you made a good connection, you receive one or more sensations:

> tingling sensation on your skin (hands and head)
> warm feeling over your body
> a slight breeze that is either cool or warm

You might receive impressions of symbolic images, geometrical patterns or pictures of real events that the tree has experienced in its time-this includes odors and scents.

If you choose to have this open and aware experience with one tree, then you realize that you are developing various levels of sensitivity to the trees' reality and your own form of reality with nature. Again record your experience, but this time in your journal and Book of Shadows. Record the date, moon sign and sun sign. By doing so you will be able to sense and bring to yourself a greater respect for nature and realize every part of creation has information that can be tapped when the seeker is ready,

MEDITATION ROOM

Find a quiet place to sit comfortably.

Close your eyes and relax by inhaling through the nose and exhaling through the mouth-do this three or four times.

Now do all of the inhaling and exhaling through the nose in a gentle manner without any pauses. In your mind you are going to build your own meditation room.

First, in a detailed manner build a table. You can decorate by adding colors and floral images. You can even give the table texture. Now place whatever you want on the table, such as inspirational book, a plant, gemstone and candles. You are at this point ready to go on a journey around the room.

While you are in your room, stand up and look around. Look and see if there are any windows, doors, book shelves. Look to see what the walls are made of. Whether the bookshelves are wooden or of another material. Perhaps you have a rug or pictures on the walls. See what you can find. Take your time. Each time you do this exercise, add something new.

When you are done, remember your experience. Then open your eyes.

DRAGON MEDITATION

Sit comfortably, relaxed, with your back straight.

Close your eyes and take 3 or 4 deep breaths.

See yourself in the countryside near the base of a mountain. As you walk, you notice the entrance to a large cave.

A friendly dragon comes out and sees you. It comes over to you and asks if you would like to go for a flight. Look carefully at the dragon. What color is it? What shape or form? Is it a young or old dragon? Does it seem fast or slow? See what else you can notice.

Thank the dragon for the offer and accept.

Climb on its back and get comfortable. You will be safe.

You can pet it, tickle it, even hug it. Whatever the Dragon feels comfortable with. Remember, it is an ancient being. Although it is serious and wise, it is still friendly.

See the dragon open its wings and fly into the sky. As you look down, what do you see? Look at all of nature. Do you see trees, ponds, lakes, meadows? What type of scene? Or is the dragon flying over snowy mountains? It can go anywhere in the world and into any area or any realm.

Pay close attention to detail as you fly. Take your time, notice everything.

Are you relaxed and watching or directing where to go?

When you are finished, tell the dragon thank you and you want to go back to where you both started the journey.

When you arrive, thank it again. Say good-bye as it goes back to its cave.

Walk back to where you started.

Slowly open your eyes.

This meditation puts you in touch with nature and points out where you feel comfortable (i.e., lake, mountain, ocean) and what you like (i.e., plants, trees, snow).

TREASURE CHEST MEDITATION

To find your magickal tool. Sword, knife, cup, feather or whatever your strongest power tool is at this time.

Sit comfortably. Relax by inhaling through the nose and exhaling through the mouth a few times. Go back to breathing in your normal manner. Close your eyes.

See a mountain before you with a large cave.

Start to walk into the cave. As you walk, you notice it is lit by the stones on the cave walls. They are shiny and bright.

You walk into a round cavern with a lake in the center. You see another entrance at the opposite side of the cavern and walk along the edge of the lake until you get there.

Once there, you walk through to a large cavern. It is brightly lit from an opening at the top. In the center of the cavern you see a large Treasure Chest.

Look at all the details. Is it wood or steel? Gold or straw? What color is it? Is it decoratively carved or plain? When you have all the details, go up to it.

Open the lid and see what tool is inside for magickal use? Once you take it out, look at the details. Remember them for later.

You will bring this back with you, so close the lid to the chest.

Holding your new tool, retrace your steps until you are back where you started. Out from this cave to the first cavern with the lake. Around the lake to the entrance. Back to the outdoors.

Then slowly open your eyes.

Bio

Rev. Maria D'Andrea, MsD, D.D., DRH. is an internationally known professional psychic from Hungary. She is an ordained minister & pastoral counselor, occultist, hypnotherapist, author, lecturer, teacher & shaman. Some of her abilities include rune casting, tarot, trance states, séance, past lives, healing, psychometry, numerology, Kirlian photography, parapsychology, astral projection, Er Mei Therapy, Qi Gong and Tai Chi. Rev. Maria is well-known for teaching Psychic & Spiritual Development. She has been a guest speaker & lecturer at various Metaphysical organizations throughout the country. She is the founder of the Sylvan Society; The PSI Esoteric Guild, and Maria D'Andrea's Psychic/Metaphysical Programs. She's a member of the NY-NJ Psychic Guild; honorary member of the Tuscarora Indian Tribe; Hungarian Writers Guild; L.I. Dowsing Assoc.; Ghost Research Society; A.R.E and A.A.H. long list of accomplishments includes having appeared on television, radio and both cable & satellite broadcasts. She also lectures and speaks at various places, such as universities and organizations. Rev. Maria has also had numerous books & articles published. She is currently founder of The D' Andrea Institute of Esoteric Studies.

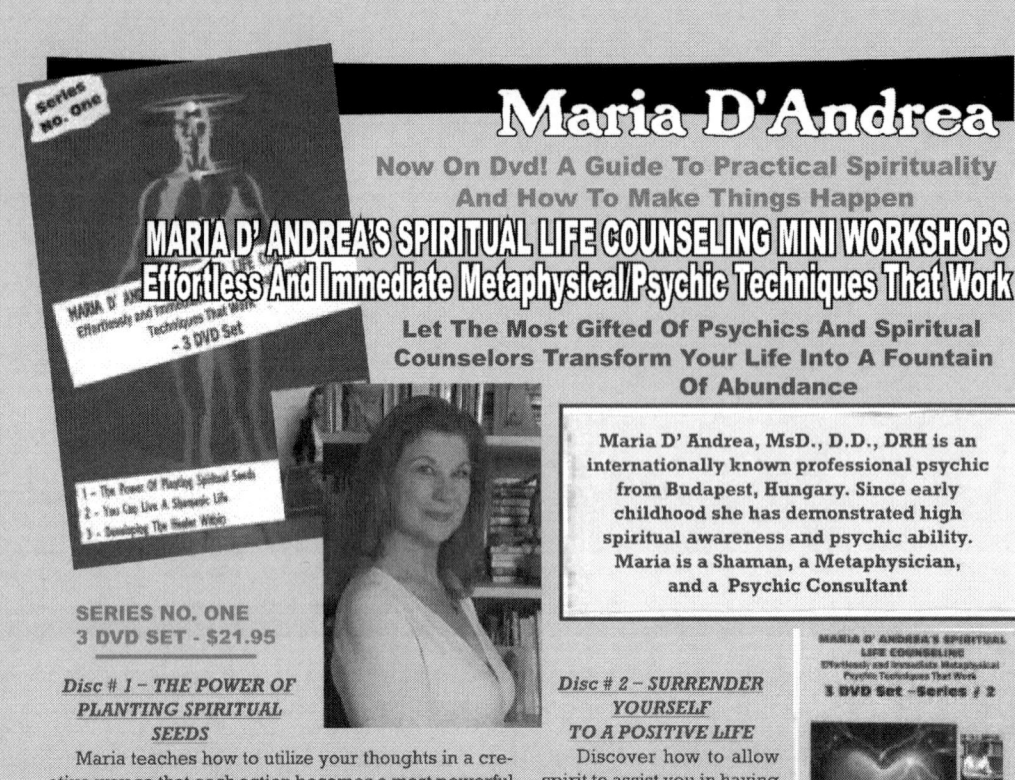

Maria D'Andrea

Now On Dvd! A Guide To Practical Spirituality And How To Make Things Happen

MARIA D' ANDREA'S SPIRITUAL LIFE COUNSELING MINI WORKSHOPS
Effortless And Immediate Metaphysical/Psychic Techniques That Work

Let The Most Gifted Of Psychics And Spiritual Counselors Transform Your Life Into A Fountain Of Abundance

Maria D' Andrea, MsD., D.D., DRH is an internationally known professional psychic from Budapest, Hungary. Since early childhood she has demonstrated high spiritual awareness and psychic ability. Maria is a Shaman, a Metaphysician, and a Psychic Consultant

SERIES NO. ONE
3 DVD SET - $21.95

Disc # 1 – THE POWER OF PLANTING SPIRITUAL SEEDS

Maria teaches how to utilize your thoughts in a creative way so that each action becomes a most powerful tool for change. This is an excellent DVD to create positive transformations in your life.

Disc # 2 — YOU CAN LEARN TO LIVE A SHAMANIC LIFE

One of the many exercises in this DVD is trusting your first instinct. Experience a journey from beginner to master and tap into hidden knowledge so your ordinary life turns into a shamanic one.

Disc # 3 – DEVELOPING THE HEALER WITHIN YOU

Discover the hidden healer within. Here are the basic principles that allows anyone to become self empowered in the healing arts. Use for your own well being and the health of your loved ones.

SERIES NO. TWO
3 DVD SET - $21.95

Disc # 1 – ATTRACTING RELATIONSHIPS

Maria teaches how to draw more positive relationships in today's world. Learn the importance of applying ancient methods to enhance your opportunities. She also explains the power of colors, gemstones and astrological periods that are best for women and men.

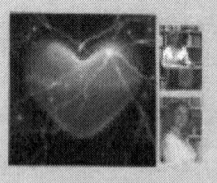

Disc # 2 – SURRENDER YOURSELF TO A POSITIVE LIFE

Discover how to allow spirit to assist you in having a more exciting life. Maria teaches the importance of releasing yourself from the past, while empowering you so that you can create your future as the present moment.

Disc # 3 – ANGELS AND THE FALL

As a Hungarian spiritual and psychic metaphysician, Maria explains the various angels and how they can assist us. She reveals the meaning and importance of shielding to assist in working with these all powerful beings. Maria shows you how to work with Archangel Ariel and Zavael with specific techniques. This DVD helps to calm the storm in your life and to create a more positive being.

VERY SPECIAL OFFER
ALL 6 DVDs JUST $39.00 + $5 S/H
ORDER FROM:
Timothy Beckley • Box 753
New Brunswick, NJ 08903
credit card order hot line:
732-602-3407

IMAGINE RECEIVING MONEY JUST BY USING THE POWERS OF YOUR MIND!

Let Maria D'Andrea Tell You How To Turn Your Dreams Into Cash— And Become A Virtual Human MONEY MAGNET

Want A New Home, Or Pay Off An Existing Mortgage?

Would you like to go on an exotic "dream" vacation with someone who is sexy or your true soul mate?

Want To Sell The Items Laying Around In Your Garage Or Attic For BIG CASH! Just like on TV's *Pawn Stars*?

Interested In Picking A "Large Prize" Lottery Ticket, Or Winning At The Tables Or Slots In "Vegas?"

Tired Of Seeing Everyone Else Wearing The "Bling?" – Diamonds May Be A Girls Best Friend, But Who Cares About Anyone Else When That Fabulous Stone Could Just As Easily Be On Your Finger.

Money Is Just Another Object – You Can Learn To Collect Dollars Just As You Would Collect Anything Else As A "Hobby."

Inspired by the *Heavenly Light* here are spells that anyone can learn to execute.

Use herbs, candles and gemstones to create prosperity! Have talismans and amulets help do the work for you! Here are dozens of ways to bring Good Luck into your life!

NEW - JUST OUT!
Hop on the path to prosperity when you utilize the easy to practice empowerments in *HEAVEN SENT MONEY SPELLS – DIVINELY INSPIRED FOR YOUR WEALTH* by Maria D' Andrea for just $21.95 + $5 S/H

Born in Budapest, Maria D' Andrea, an internationally known professional psychic, occultist, hypnotist, minister, teacher and radio/television personality, for the first time passes on ancient knowledge as well as her own formulas for being FINANCIALLY SUCCESSFUL! "The forces of nature are here to be worked with in a positive way," the gifted seers has stated. "This is information that has been passed down by word of mouth from the ancient wise known by titles such as magi, shamans, priestesses, elders, and sages."

Also Available-
TRIPLE THE POWER OF THE SPELLS IN THIS BOOK WITH YOUR PERSONAL. . .

Third Pentacle of the Sun Talisman This authentic replica of an ancient talisman used by the prophets of old grants you the ability to acquire immense riches, glory and renown. Measuring 1" in diameter, this potent amulet comes on a black satin cord.

Priced to sell at $25 by itself, you may order Maria's new Heaven Sent Money Spells book and the Pentacle of the Sun Talisman for just $42.00 + $5.00 S/H

Order From – Timothy Beckley
Box 753 • New Brunswick, NJ 08903
Credit Card hotline 732 602-3407
PayPal MRUFO8@hotmail.com

Printed in Great Britain
by Amazon